OUT NOW

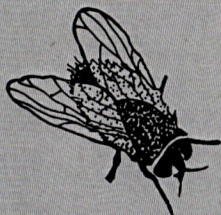

CW01394565

(sic)

Coughing up popular
culture and poking
about in it with a pencil

Available from AK Press or from all good bookshops
ISBN 1-900672-01-4   £4.95

Box TR666, Armle
email: sic@chu
http://www.chu

SIC

Contents

Published by Book Press ISBN 1-900672-01-4
Anti-copyright September 2002

SIC

> **"The New Left sprang, a predestined pissed-off child, from Elvis's gyrating pelvis"**
> **—Jerry Rubin, *DO IT!***

When we first started talking about putting *Sic* together we had Alex Trocchi's Project Sigma in our heads. In the sixties Trocchi sent out a list of artists, radicals, musicians, poets and the generally belligerent. It was just a list, a straightforward and simple roll call of people he thought were in some way connected, and everybody on the list got a copy of it. Surprisingly, Trocchi's list really was part of expanding the movement. A poet and a heroin addict, Trocchi organised the poetic equivalent of seeing the Sex Pistols at the 100 Club, the gig at the Royal Albert Hall in 1965 where 7,000 people gathered and Jeff Nuttall painted himself blue and collapsed when he forgot to leave a patch for the skin to breathe, Ginsberg insisted on people chanting the phrase 'You are not alone', and Adrian Mitchell said 'Tell Me Lies about Vietnam' and poetry was stolen away from Betjeman and linked to liberation and revolution. Apparently, it was the night people realised that there were thousands of others who felt just like them.

Seattle was important for the same underlying reason but what made Seattle a landmark wasn't numbers but difference: trade unionists walked next to artists dressed as turtles, church groups linked up with anarchists and Brazilian peasants. It was the massing of all these people under a broad banner which marked out Seattle, and the fact that they didn't have to abolish their differences to come together. We're not trying to recreate the night at the Albert Hall or publish our own little paper Seattle but we are trying to put engaged artists and activists in the same space and capture some of the

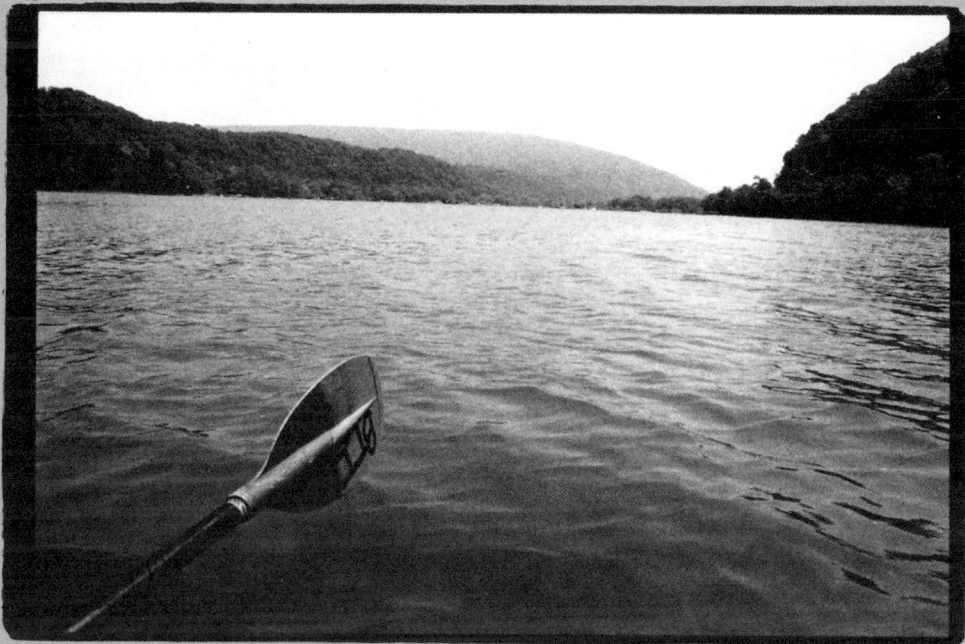

ideas which are tossed around when history speeds up... and it's speeding up now.

If there's one theme which is repeated throughout *Sic*'s interviews and articles it's that creative and political leaps forward are always the result of collective ideas. As Jake Black from Alabama 3 points out, punk was life-changing for him because of the interaction between working and middle class kids, while Jon Savage says that when the Stones, the Beatles and the Sex Pistols were at their most productive they were surrounded by artists, designers, film-makers, avant garde musicians and radicals. The album or the book or the rally might have one name on the masthead but any leap forward is a result of collective effort. The internet, e-mail and mass communication have made working with others easier than ever before; the flipside to globalisation is that it's possible, even easy, to talk to anti-capitalists in Mexico, Italy and Argentina and work out what we can learn from them. *Sic* isn't a pop magazine with politics or a political magazine with pop: we inhabit the territory where these worlds collide. What we're interested in is the point of convergence where sex and drugs and rock'n'roll meet struggle and art and literature. We've tried to talk to people who understand that culture always reflects or repudiates the times. *Sic* is an irony-free zone and we're looking for collaborators for subsequent issues. ✖

sic@chumba.demon.co.uk

Don't wet your pants. It's only a fucking car.

Just A Car

With a brand new vocabulary of meaningless buzzwords like JTS injection and optional infotelemac sytem, coupled with wholly inappropriate adjectives such as exhilarating and breathtaking, you might think we're boasting about something truly special. Our over-use of words like freedom, individuality, power and expression might suggest something more than a silvery-coloured motor vehicle. But no, it's only a car.

The new car. It's a car.

ONLY A CAR

A Car

Sic **takes a raincheck at the checkout — this week it's a Buenos Aires store where "everything must go"**

Nappies aren't just a sound move financially — practically they'll also come in handy as emergency bandaging, sanitary protection and makeshift sandbags

With its slow-release carbohydrates, pasta is an excellent source of energy, although a wholewheat variety would provide slightly more fibre and help to avoid the kind of blockages that have blighted social movements over the last few years

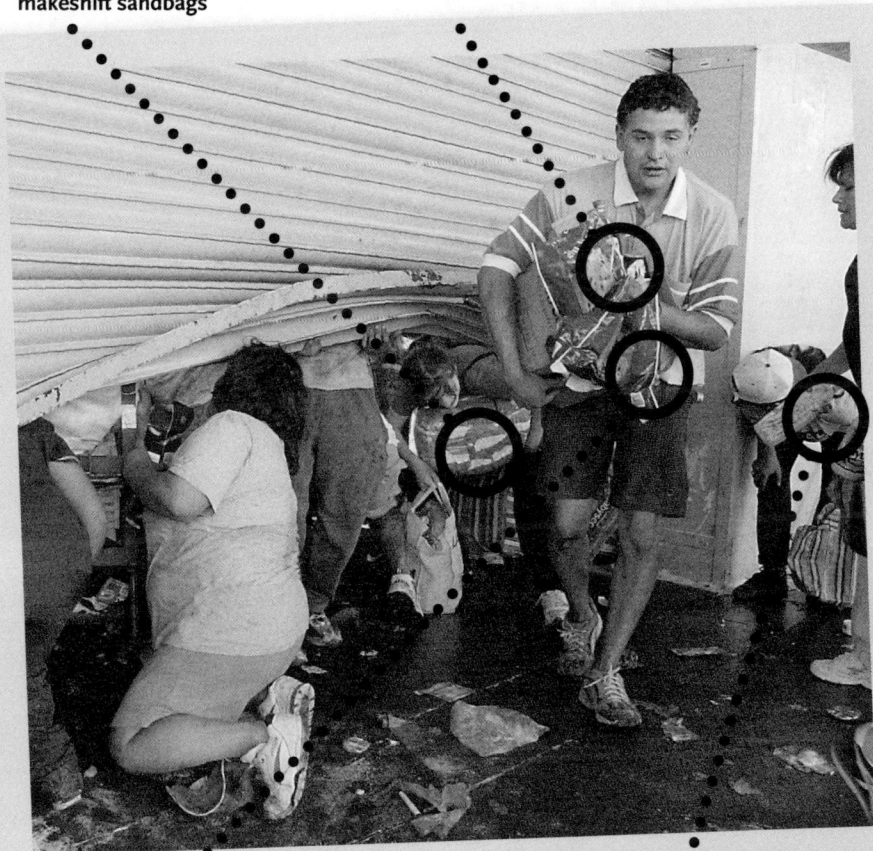

Frozen chips are a crowd-pleaser but remember that too much fatty food will play havoc with your complexion and may make people think you come from up North

It's always important to maintain liquid intake during any kind of social upheaval, and water is the sensible choice here

Mark Thomas

NEED TO KNOW

What was the first record you ever bought?

The first LP I ever bought was Emerson Lake and Palmer – *Tarkus*. I'm sorry, I'm so, so sorry – I was only 11.

What was your first job?

Sweeping up shavings for my dad when I was eight. 10p an hour.

Do you know a line of poetry by heart? What is it?

Blake – *London*.

> I wandered down by the chartered streets
> Near where the chartered Thames doth flow
> And saw in every face I met
> Marks of weakness, marks of woe
> In every voice, in every ban
> The mind-forged manacles I hear...

Fuck, I'll have to go and look it up now, I can't remember it properly...

What qualities do you respect?

Tenacity, loyalty and righteousness.

Who or what do you have absolutely no respect for?

The stock market and the Labour Party.

Who or what has had the biggest influence on your life so far?

A couple of really good teachers, Tony Green and Duncan Noel Patton, Noam Chomsky, punk, my dad, the miners' strike, Jenny Landreth, the legend of Lenny Bruce, Alexei Sayle, Tony Allen and Bob Boyton, two comics who opened all the doors for me, Nick and Kerim from the Ilisu Dam Campaign, loads of things really.

Who or what makes you laugh?

My family. My little boy Charlie, 7, is very funny and can reduce me to tears when he mimes country and western songs. Other than that, the Simpsons and comics like Rob Newman, Mark Steel and Jeremy Hardy are my favourites.

Which was the biggest bare-faced lie ever told to you?

An arms dealer said he was only joking when I told him I was recording his conversation about selling guns to Zimbabwe thus breaking the EU embargo on arms sales and Finnish law. He was Finnish so breaking Finnish law would have had consequences for him.

What's the biggest bare-faced lie you've ever told?

I once told an Indonesian Major General that he should trust me completely, that not one word he said would go further than the two of us.

What keeps you awake at night?

My children.

Who or what gives cause for optimism?

Too many things to write here, but essentially people's ability to organise and fight in the face of adversity. The imagination that people innately have to solve problems and fuck off authority.

What sort of drunk are you?
Bad, which is why I don't drink.

Which films have you watched more than three times?
Citizen Kane, The Rear Window, Passport to Pimlico, Hard Boiled, Kind Hearts and Coronets, Raining Stones, When We Were Kings, Riff Raff.

Which two books would you take to a desert island?
The biggest Dickens going, I've never read him. My Uncle David was a miner who joined the merchant navy and was an inveterate gambler, drunk, trouble-maker and womaniser. He read and re-read every single Dickens novel. He continually mocked me when he was alive for never having read Dickens. So I feel I ought to. The second book would be 'Gourmet Cooking on a Desert Island'.

What do you think of reality TV?
Reality and television are not regular bedfellows. Anything called reality TV is going to have very little to do with reality or at least most people's idea of it. So it is not going to be ground-breaking stuff. I do watch *Big Brother* occasionally, I don't mind gently switching off from the day to it, but I could get the same effect watching fish in a tank frankly.

Where were you when Princess Diana died and what was your reaction?
My mate phoned to tell me Sunday morning and my first reaction was to laugh... actually it was my second and third reaction too! ✖

Deputy Assistant Chief Constable Roy Nail answers your questions

Q Dear Roy, what is canteen culture?
A Look, the PC brigade likes to make a song and dance over this but you have to understand policing is a stressful job and banter is an important part of winding down. We all have our nicknames and I don't go running to the race relations industry if officers call me "Geordie", "Guv" or "Sir". But if one of us tells an Asian officer, "Why don't you take the curry boat back to Wogland, you Paki cunt?" everyone cries, "Racist!"

Q Dear Roy, what is zero tolerance?
A The idea comes from America, where tolerance is now down to about 1%.

Q Dear Roy, why do so many innocent people end up in jail?
A Innocent people are easier to catch. They're not expecting anything. Look, if we restricted our inquiries to the guilty, we'd never get anywhere. Take the bloke we did for whacking that blonde bird Jan Dildo off the telly. Two years arsing

SICNOTES

The only person I can think of who I really rate is Richard M. Stallman. He's a computer programmer and the founder of the Free Software movement (www.fsf.org). The purpose of this rather boring-sounding org is to ensure the availability of software, which we can all use, whose source code is open and which is developed and improved by those who believe in the project.

Stallman is the inventor of an editing programme called emacs, and has contributed a variety of other free applications to the open source operating system known as GNU/Linux. He is extremely dogmatic, opinionated and long-haired. He's one of those blokes who, if you say 'god willing,' will reply 'there is no god.' People like this can be annoying, but in the case of Stallman we have to honour him for – almost single-handedly, at times – fighting the good fight against corporate control-freakers like Microsoft and Apple (who would like to be Microsoft, and are part-owned by them) and their inferior, expensive and secretive software.

around looking for someone guilty and where did it get us? People want results. We needed someone violent, obsessed with militaria and with a dysfunctional attitude to women. Jim Davidson was booked for our Christmas party so we went for monkey boy. And look at it this way. Better that a hundred innocent people are wrongly convicted than that one go free. That's the real miscarriage of justice.

Q Roy, how does being a born again Christian help in your work?

A Let's get one thing straight. Jesus was guilty. Fact. And he was not ill-treated. He fell on the nails when they were putting him in the van. So my Christianity is not about the man or his ideas. He wasn't a Christian anyway. He was a Jew. Fact.

Q Dear Roy, how is an unarmed police force able to shoot so many people?

A Once again the politically correct lobby seeks to undermine confidence in the police service as a whole. Perhaps you would like to know that being shot by the police is still one of the safest ways of being killed. People shot by us have dropped very rapidly, one in the head normally does it and the number is very small, especially as a proportion of the total number of people we kill. Guns are only part of it, let me tell you. All deaths are immediately and thoroughly rubber-stamped by the Police Complaints Authority, and the families get to have a weep and moan at the inquest. Yes, mistakes have been made in the past, but we in the Police Federation are proud of our traditions.

Q Dear Roy, what is your opinion of gay officers?

A Although personally I find their practices repugnant, especially shopping and baking, which to a bluff northerner like me are mothers' work, intellectually I have no objection. The only thing I'd stick up another's man's arse is my truncheon, but each to his own. However, when it comes to serving officers, there's a problem. Being in the front line of the war against crime involves a lot of intimacy. Officers routinely shower together with larks a-plenty, so how's an officer supposed to feel about his colleagues if he's not sure how they feel about being felt? Horseplay is one thing, man-milking another.

Q Dear Roy, do too many people get off on technicalities?

A Absolutely. Lawyers are poring over every bit of paperwork to find some "discrepancy", "inconsistency" or evidence pointing at the real culprit. Woebetide the honest copper whose notes are not "contemporaneous". But how's he supposed to write down a verbatim confession with one hand behind the suspect's back? ✖

Who cares about software? You should, because it is running on the computers that control many aspects of your life. Ignore it at your peril: Blunkett and Ashcroft won't. But Stallman knows a free operating system is part of a larger battle – hence the Free Software movement's battle against DVD encryption and the attempts by Microsoft and repressive government to dictate the uses you can put your computer to; and their attempts – already in train – to make operating systems and software INFORM ON THEIR USERS! Check Stallman and the FSF out. You can download free software from the internet for nowt, or order a whole system on CD rom (try Red Hat or Mandrake or Slackware, or if you're really computer-literate the completely non-profit Debian) for a couple of quid from cheepbytes.com or similar. And you can learn more about 'copyleft' – a radical alternative to patent and copyright law, which encourages you to recycle and improve on others' work.

Alex Cox

Artifice for art's sake

Sic **talks to rock'n'roll legend and quick change artist El Vez**

"No matter what people say about you, son, you know who you are and that's all that matters"
Gladys Presley to her son, Elvis

"It's not who you are but who you could be... " El Vez is a 21st century version of the old black and white movie stars and like Rudolph Valentino before him: it's not what El Vez is but what he appears to be which matters. He is a multi-ethnic, multi-cultural, multi-costumed, revolutionary Mexican Elvis. He looks like a pretty pick-up artist with a little bit of every cool icon worked in to the moves. El Vez is the dream made flesh: living proof that anybody and everybody can be a star and that nothing is fixed – not even colour or sexuality. Like a Woolworth print he's a copy of a work of art but as El Vez says: "Through imitation you can find realities."

"What should I call you?" I ask before the interview begins, "Am I talking to El Vez or Robert?" "Robert," he says in a voice that's low, American and serious. El Vez is higher, has a Spanish inflection and comes across as a firecracker about to go off.

Robert Lopez is the former singer of the seminal LA punk band the Zeros. He metamorphosed into El Vez while working as a curator at a Mexican folk/pop art gallery, La Luz De Jesus Gallery, on Melrose Avenue in Los Angeles. "I had curated a show on Elvis, and we had Elvis impersonators and a whole month of Elvis-themed events," he says "After seeing the Elvis impersonator, I thought I could do better." As a dare he went off to an Elvis Tribute Week in Memphis, where he won an Elvis impersonator contest at Bad Bob's Vapours.

El Vez doesn't impersonate Elvis; he

translates him and a host of other pop references so that the songs are full of rage, observation, optimism and humour. Pop classics are cleverly and lovingly bastardised so that Ricky Martin's 'La Vida Loca' and Rod Stewart's 'Maggie May' end up in a set which plays with cultural identity, lambasts deaths on the Mexican border whilst celebrating the Zapatistas and sexuality. This isn't about authenticity: "The whole idea was to take US icons and subvert them. It's the Duchamp idea of putting a moustache on the Mona Lisa. El Vez is an American icon because to be Mexican is American, El Vez is a blank canvas on which to paint grand ideas."

Rock'n'roll has always been a way to transcend the limits of society and ourselves. We're all of us more than one person, with more dimensions and contradictions than job descriptions, star signs and stereotyping allows. El Vez enables Robert to break out of the restrictions of cultural definitions and sexual labels: "I'm gay and El Vez is straight," says Robert. "It's rock and roll sexuality, like Little Richard and the New York Dolls. Sexuality in a rock and roll context doesn't have the same barriers... and what I do with El Vez is all impersonation. I'm not Elvis, I'm really from San Diego, I'm not Mexican, I'm not actually straight. It's all impersonation: as El Vez I have a mask – not a real one, just a tiny little moustache mask – but masks can be liberating."

In El Vez's universe the American dream isn't colour-coded. El Vez tries to force America to honour the 'Bring me your poor, your tired and your hungry' line that immigrants sailed past on their way into Ellis Island. Like the Soviet workers in the old revolutionary posters he's gazing into a future that the rest of us can't see. For all his lines about segregated ghettos El Vez loves America;

the kitsch, the malls and the everyday art of Jesus as a living room rug. He's not a poster boy for capitalism with the Fordian idea of no real freedom but a new fridge, a new car and a place in the suburbs. El Vez's America is a place where everybody can become a star no matter what size, shape or colour they are.

"El Vez believes that; I don't. El Vez is more optimistic than me. He thinks everybody can become King and go for the gusto. He's romantic about ideas and I am more cynical. It's optimism peppered with intelligence. He believes in the possibilities of revolution and the people moving forward. El Vez believes in the Cesar Chavez idea that every worker is an organiser. I don't believe that. Still, it's possible to hold these two dissenting ideas in your brain at the same time. It's a very Mexican idea, like the Day of the Dead, we celebrate life by making fun of death."

> "What I do with El Vez is all impersonation. I'm not Elvis, I'm really from San Diego, I'm not Mexican, I'm not actually straight. It's all impersonation"

The beauty of El Vez is that an act which could so easily be a one trick pony is multi-dimensional. Few entertainers would dare to get a room full of white kids, LA Latinos and middle aged couples all shouting together: "Say it loud! I'm Brown and I'm proud!" Robert explains: "The trip to El Vez-ness was a search for identity. How brown can I be? What are my roots? When you come to an El Vez show, you walk away proud to be a Mexican, even when you're not."

El Vez gigs are full of life-affirming statements, gospel testifying 'I admit I have sinned... I voted Republican... I sold crack to the contras!' but there's still a seam of fury running through the songs and the parodies. "It's a different sort of anger from my days in the Zeros. Teenage rage is a lot different to the anger you feel later, it's more about hormones and immediate circumstances and later it's more about the way the world works. Punk was more angsty, more freaky, there was more alienation. We were the freaks, the creeps, it was us against the world. We were entertaining ourselves more than people."

He's an old fashioned entertainer, he has the charisma of a medicine man who could sell you almost anything. Audiences like him, can relate to him, there's a puppy dog warmth about him that Robert doesn't have. Robert is cooler; more considered. His band, the Memphis Mariachis and his backing singers the Elvettes, are plugged into the same socket and the live shows are a high speed chase through the annals of pop culture with a costume change at every pit stop.

"I rob the musical bank of everything... I'll rob the Beatles and take one of David Johanssen's moves and add a touch of Thin White Duke. Taking from all over just creates a bigger collage and it becomes something different when it's all placed together. I blur the line between what is satire and what is having a laugh. People get religion, satire, politics all done in the context of a rock'n'roll concert. Some people come along and see it as a reason to drink tequila margaritas and that's alright too, there's room for them all."

The reason that an El Vez

congregation is so inclusive is that there's no element of studied reserve. He's willing to be larger than life and risk making a fool out of himself which he never does, and the humour means he's as palatable to mainstream America as he is to the hybrid audiences who come to see him perform. How many other political popstars have managed to get their face on a US stamp? When the US Post Office put out a special Elvis stamp, they got El Vez to officiate at the unveiling. He brought his own stamp along and suggested they manufacture that too, and they did. Last year he put himself up for political office, using the platform to criticise the lack of choice in organised politics.

"Voting these days is about choosing the lesser of two evils. I say we create a brand-new evil. It will give new people a chance. In a time when the left is leaning to the right, and the right is shifting to the left, it's hard to tell the difference anymore (especially when you consider the two candidates). Brown Party National Convention occurs every time we have a show."

El Vez has got himself ordained as a minister and plans are in the pipeline for special wedding shows. His last record was 'Boxing With God' which was based on a play which Al Green did in the seventies called 'It Takes A Short Left Arm To Box With God'. For the stage show he modelled himself on the smart and pretty Mexican boxer, Oscar De la Hoya, and the gigs were more about sex and celebrating the beauty of everyday objects than worshipping a deity.

"I wanted to capture that euphoric feeling of Saturday night turning into Sunday morning. It's a sort of Mexican spirituality. In my romantic idea the shrine of the Virgin of Guadalupe is built on a shopping centre with a car park, a mall and the works. It's full of the things that we use in our daily life, spirituality being wherever you are, whether you're going to the toilet, having sex or cooking. Each time you touch an everyday object it's part of a religious experience. This is the embodiment of a whole religious life, not religion hidden in some dark space, not using religion as a weapon of hate."

Rock'n'roll can be equally exciting as a vehicle for ideas or as a throwaway adrenaline rush, that's the beauty of it. Pop culture allows us to take risks, shows us avenues where we can transform ourselves. El Vez is the ultimate symbol of transformation and he loves pop culture and understands how to use it.

"There is irony in what I do, it can be beautiful, stupid, plain, simple, complicated all at the same time. Some of my lines are incredibly stupid, you wouldn't say them but it works in this context of rock'n'roll." ✖

SICNOTES

A few months ago I went to a church in a posher part of Chicago and found myself part of a standing ovation for the current lame-duck Republican governor of Illinois. Not my usual scene f'sure. He'd just made a speech explaining his decision to impose a moratorium on the death penalty in this state. Stung by accusations of corruption and hated by his own party, George Ryan's stab at a legacy appears to be the telling of truths. He freely admitted voting for the re-introduction of state executions way back when and running for office on a tough-on-crime, pro-death penalty ticket without ever having really given it any thought beyond it being a safe Republican issue; a comfy political football.

What changed his mind and why does it matter? As governor, presiding over Illinois' broken capital justice system, he was forced to think about it and with the real possibility that he might get caught sending innocent people to die – he stopped it. If someone who invested in the system can become convinced it's wrong and be shocked – by his complacency – into action then anything can happen. Inspiring really... so I stood up and clapped.

Jon Langford

Trade unionist

Arsenal fan

Straight

Irish

Teenager

Landless peasant

Green

Unemployed

Punk

Mother

Black

Web designer

HIV-positive

Clubber

Refugee

Working class

Self-employed

Snowboarder

Anti-capitalist

Nurse

IDENTITY = DOMINATION

How to be an artist

by Bill Drummond

taken from *How To Be An Artist*
published by the Penkiln Burn 2002

FOR SALE

A SMELL OF SULPHUR IN THE WIND
Richard Long

$20,000

'Do you want a hand in with your bits Bill?'

'No thanks. I like doing it myself but I wouldn't mind a cup of tea.'

So I entered the place with my rolled-up carpet on my shoulder. I asked the people to move back as I did my by now well-practised unrolling.

'We have a kettle but no plug Bill. Do you have a screwdriver we could use to take the plug off the projector to put on the kettle?'

'It's OK, I'll settle for a glass of water.' I got my other bits in. Leant them against the wall and then I began.

'Good evening. My name is Bill Drummond, and I'm here this evening to make a sales pitch. What I would like to sell is...' and I was off, swaggering around my carpet, lifting my merchandise up at irreverent angles for all to see. My tongue was silver, my anecdotes burnished, my self-deprecating asides as finely tuned as Mika Hakkinen's Mercedes/McLaren.

The crowd went from first-year art students up to lecturers considering what to do with early retirement. What was good about this bunch was that it wasn't just the usual couple of cocky lads who had a lot to say – just as many of the women were cutting in with their remarks and questions.

'However much you wrap it up, however much you say or don't say, you're falling into the same trap as Richard Long. However pure his initial impetus, it is all negated by the commodification of his work. You are, almost by your own admission, on the same road.'

'But...' But I can't remember how I answered that one.

'All this about not knowing what you had bought is somewhat disingenuous of you. You know exactly what you bought and you don't like what it says about you. And now you want shot of it.'

'So what have I bought?'

'Porn.'

'I have never felt the need to buy porn in my life.'

'Well anybody who buys art not as an investment or to impress friends or cheer the place up a bit is buying porn.'

'Porn. I'm not getting a hard on, are you?'

'You know what I mean. You are buying into something because you can't do it or get it yourself. You wouldn't buy porn if you could get all the perverted sexual kicks you desired for free with willing collaborators. There'd be no need. By buying this art you are buying into an experience at one remove. You are paying Richard Long to do it for you while you toss yourself off at his conceptual flights of fancy. Anthony D'Offay, the pimp; Richard Long, the whore; and you're the John. The trouble is you've sussed it and this Smell of Sulphur in the Wind is just a smutty magazine with the pages stuck together and now you want shot of it.'

This was getting good and then a man at the back cut in with a very simple and straightforward question, 'Do you own any other art?' A yes or no answer would have sufficed but I sidestepped the thrust of his question by giving the answer, 'Only a few bits and pieces by friends.' The trouble with this answer is the word 'friend', a word that can mean different things to different people.

As a person who prefers to spend as much time as possible in my own head, I've never quite been able to give up the childish habit of having fantasy friends. One of those friends is Monet. I like to chat with him in his garden while he paints his pond.

'Look Claude, why don't you give the painting a rest today? By my reckoning there is a giant pike lurking under those lily pads. What do you say we get ourselves a couple of rods and go after him?'

'You don't understand Bill, do you?'

And then there is me and Rothko.

'Look Mark, this stuff you're doing is going nowhere, it's boring. Cut out some magazine ads for Hoovers and Coca-Cola and stick them onto your dreary washes of colour. You never know, it might be an artistic breakthrough. If you carry on like this it will drive you to suicide.'

'Suicide, that's a good idea Bill, that should seal my mythical status.'

'Fuck the myth-making, lighten up Mark. Let's get down the Cedar for a few beers.'

I do have some friends and I have got some art at home.

But anyway, more of that later. I got in my story about how I used to be based in Aberdeen back in 1974 when I was briefly an apprentice trawlerman on a

WARRANTY

Bill Drummond warrants that attached to this card is a 1/20,000 fraction of the artwork, A Smell Of Sulphur In The Wind by the artist Richard Long.

Bill Drummond warrants that as long as stocks of these fragments are still for sale, their value will remain at $1.00 each, and that once all 20,000 fragments have been sold, he will take the 20,000 dollar bills to Iceland in an oak box and bury it at the centre of the stone circle featured in the photographic content of the original artwork. (see reverse).

The buyer is welcome to bury as many portions as they wish and will be contacted by e-mail when all 20,000 have been sold with the date when the fees will be buried.

The buyer will inform penkilnburn.com/shop of any changes in their e-mail address and will be kept informed of any new developments concerning this undertaking.

The buyer will be able to visit penkiln-burn.com/shop in order to monitor the progress of sales and to view the exact location of their fragment using the given grid reference.

Good luck.

The Seller: B. ____ The Buyer: Sic People

Grid reference: 6 Across / 57 Down

FOR SALE

A SMELL OF SULPHUR IN THE WIND
Richard Long

$20,000

U.K.A.E.A.
THIS NOTICE MARKS THE BOUNDARY
OF
THE DOUNREAY NUCLEAR LICENCED SITE
IN ACCORDANCE WITH THE NUCLEAR INSTALLATIONS ACT 1965
UNAUTHORISED ENTRY PROHIBITED

OCTOBER 1990

boat working the northern waters. The show went well. The applause was genuine. Various offers were made to join the throng at various bars. As I packed up, all offers of help were politely turned down. This too was all part of the show. Weave that myth boy, weave that myth. Two women offered to help. This was two women separate from each other. My ego felt ten feet tall. Me need porn? Not likely son. With a rolled-up carpet like mine why would I ever need a dirty mag?

And I was off into the darkening sky in search of those northern lights and a single bed in some wayside inn.

But I got lost off Commercial Street, down by the docks. The street was empty but for a young lady with long blonde hair and micro-skirt. I slowed down to check her out, see if she was worth propositioning. My proposition was to be, 'Do you mind holding one of these "For Sale" placards love, while I take a photo of you?' But when I screwed up my eyes to get a better look at her, to see if she was worth the proposition, I realised I didn't have my specs on.

Instant U-turn back up the guilty streets, around the bend and into Justice Street. Relief, there were still people clearing up and drinking the last dregs of wine. My specs were waiting for me faithfully by the glass of water.

Off across town again. Behind the drawn curtains I could imagine fathers reading their sons a bedtime story. 'Once upon a time, a long time ago there was a football manager who managed the lads up at Pittodrie Park. Those lads in red were the true Dons, they brought back European silver, something that Rangers have never done, never mind how many times they have won the league.'

'But Dad, why doesn't he still manage the reds?'

'He does son, they just happen not to be our reds.'

'But whose reds are they Dad?'

'Manchester United's, son.'

Poor boy, his dad reads him the same story every night and every night he wonders if he could ever tell his dad that he secretly supports Manchester United.

I stopped on a tree-lined street to stick up a placard outside a granite house with the curtains shut in honour of the Don's glory days. I stuck up another one, hoping the snap would capture the last lingering light of the day. This one was in honour of Billy Lyndsey, an Aberdonian and follower of the Dons. Billy was the first in our class to jack in the sixth form. His first weekly wage packet was four pounds, nineteen shillings and sixpence (£4/19/6d), as a trainee quantity surveyor.

He was also the first of us to father a child.

The A96 out of town. I was hoping to make Inverness before I turned in but just a couple of miles further up the road and I was falling asleep at the wheel. They may not have been the Northern Lights, but the lights of Aberdeen Airport looked mighty fine to me. They drew me in and, waving my credit card, I checked into the biggest airport hotel on offer, ordered a half-bottle of Cabernet Sauvignon and some seafood pasta dish on room service, tried to phone Sallie to see how she and the family were but fell asleep before my meal and wine arrived.

I woke up. It was still dark. The hum of the air conditioning began to frighten me. There was a voice in my head.

'Do you own any other art? I said, do you own any other art? Mr Drummond, are you listening? DO YOU OWN ANY OTHER ART?'

'Yes, I'm listening.'

'Well do you? And don't give me any of that bollocks about Monet and Rothko. You don't have imaginary friends, you just made that up for effect. A yes or no answer is what I require.'

'Look, didn't you read that story in 45 where I went off to buy that advert thing to cure myself of the need to buy art?'

'Yes.'

'So?'

'So you still haven't come clean with me, have you?'

'Fuck off and let me go back to sleep. I've got an early start you know.'

'Yes I know but a little birdy tells me

FOR SALE
A SMELL OF SULPHUR IN THE WIND
Richard Long
$20,000

SICNOTES

Listen. In 1985 I spent some time as resident writer in a youth custody centre (once called a borstal, now a young offenders institution, all euphemisms for a kids' prison). T.J. was about sixteen, maybe seventeen tops. He was in there for starting fires. He was a serial arsonist. The others – most of them banged up for petty crimes: drugs, TWOC-ing, burglary, shoplifting – dismissed him as a nutter.

This particular day, they were having a go at him. He didn't care. I said: "So go on then, why'd you do it?" "Fuckin 'ell," he said, "I've been in here for over a year and you're the first person to ask me that. I'll tell you."

Here's what T.J. told us. All his life he'd been in trouble. Didn't get on with his parents or his teachers or the police or the other kids around the terraced Sheffield backstreets where he lived. Always fighting. Soon he was being chucked out of his house first thing and not let back in till evening. A street kid, except no-one on the street played with him. He'd end up fighting with them or getting them into trouble. Soon, their parents wouldn't allow them to play with him anyway. He became a loner. But he was no fool. He was a bright kid. Sharper than most. You could tell.

you've got a couple of Richard Billinghams hanging in your house. Can you explain this?'

'So what?'

'So what! A lot of people think the idea of the art-buying classes spending thousands on photographs depicting the dysfunctional goings-on in the Billingham household is an abomination of taste. Hanging these pictures of fat Liz and alckie Ray on their walls for their friends to admire when they come round for a dinner party is about as sad and sick as the art market can get.'

'Of course I know that.'

'So why aren't you getting rid of these pictures as well as or at least instead of the Richard Long one? Are you afraid of what your dirty little secret tells the world about you?'

'Well firstly, I bought them as gifts for my girlfriend, Sallie, and our daughter, Tiger. They own them, I'm not in a position to sell them.'

'You're dodging the issue.'

'No I'm not. I'm just getting to it. As I've said before, I've got no on-going relationship with the Richard Long picture, it doesn't engage me. If art doesn't engage you, it has no worth. Every day the two Richard Billingham

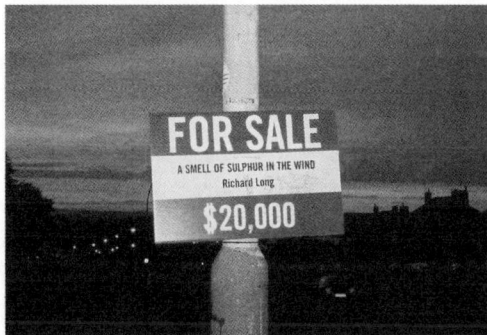

photos we have hanging in our house engage me. They work. They do their job. I'm getting my money's worth.'

'Work? Doing their job? Money's worth? Mr Drummond, what kind of far-fetched reasoning is this?'

'Every morning I come downstairs and I've got to go through our living room to get to the kitchen. On our living room wall is a big print of Liz reclining on her grubby settee in her flat somewhere in the redundant West Midlands, surveying our spacious living room somewhere in the home counties. And Liz is not some fiction in an artist's head, she is living, breathing, dealing with life, not a Henri Cartier-Bresson black and white image from a now mythical past or a chic portrait of a Nan

Maybe boredom fed the punk movement, but it ate at him. So he broke into empty warehouses and other inner city buildings abandoned by mass unemployment. He'd explore them and make his plan. Choose a target. Work out where best to set fires. When best to do it. And he'd watch the comings and goings of caretakers, cleaners and security men. Work out when the place was empty. Collect whatever he needed. Stash it all out of sight someplace in there where it was ready. Choose a ____. Work out a route for himself. Double-check everything. It all lent meaning, purpose and interest to his life. It occupied him. And then the day came. And then dusk, when he headed for his building. And after he'd lit all the fires, he'd climb the side of the valley and with a cig, watch the column of smoke thicken and blacken, the flames grow, the crowd gather, the fire engines arrive. And then he'd know that half of Sheffield would've seen what was happening, know that it'd be on the news, in the papers. And he'd sit there, light himself a second cig, survey the whole scene, and say to himself: "I did that!"

And finishing his story, he looked round at us all and said: "And, you know what? That's the best feeling in the fucking world." And suddenly none of us sat there thought he was mad. Just for that moment, arson made perfect sense. We all wanted a go. Like having your own fireworks on bonfire night, but more real. And not one of us spoke. Now that's what I call a religious experience.

Nick Toczek

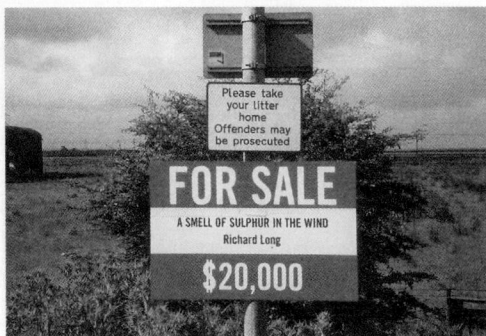

Goldin cross-dressing heroin-shooting friend, dying of aids. It's a here and now, just up the M1 thing. Liz is putting on the kettle as I put on the kettle. She is feeding her dogs and cats as I feed ours. If Liz died then there might be no reason for having her up. The force of the picture would change. It would become history, as in redundant. Like a picture of the Queen on the wall of your local British Legion – as soon as she dies it will no longer work and will have to be replaced by a picture of Charles. "The king is dead, long live the king" and all that. The fact they are both called Liz is a bonus.'

'But Mr Drummond, the commodification of someone else's misfortunes for your entertainment is as sick as contemporary art can get.'

'You said that before and anyway you are again stating the obvious. That's what gives it power. Whether Richard Billingham as the artist intended that is irrelevant. The whole notion of Richard Billingham taking pictures of his own white-trash family and selling them for a considerable profit gives this stuff more potency. Most art that gets produced is far too self-aware to work. There is very little friction within it. So often it is just a display of wit and intelligence. Most art doesn't fuck with your head. It just pats it and says, "Aren't you clever, you get it too." It's all been worked out before we

see it. Even if the artists pretend themselves to be innocent in all of this, that too is part of the game that they are selling and what we are buying.'

'You're over-stating it Drummond. There is a lot of art being made out there that isn't just a display of wit and intelligence for those who get it, to indulge in. There's still no need to go and buy the stuff.'

'Look, if you really want to know it gets worse, far worse and that's why I like it even more. I've got a friend, a photographer, whose name is Paul Graham. He saw some of Billingham's photos in a group show at the Barbican back in 1994. This was Billingham's first show outside of the West Midlands, and since leaving art school. The show was called 'Who's Looking at the Family.'

'Paul introduced himself to Billingham at the opening of this Barbican show, told him that if he was down in London again to look him up. Billingham did, and a loose working relationship evolved. Billingham had no gear, he got his photos developed at the local Boots using the cheapest film he could find. Paul had top gear. Paul introduced Billingham's work to Anthony Reynolds, the owner of the gallery that represents Paul. Reynolds recognised the commercial possibilities of Billingham's family snaps. Paul printed up Billingham's snaps to the large scale format that has become the

norm since photographs first began to be marketed as contemporary art. Photos as big as paintings to compete in the white-wall wars and all that well-documented stuff.

'Now I could have got myself some off-cuts from Paul's studio floor or even (maybe) a reject print before Paul tore it up and flung it in the bin. I could have Blu-tacked these off-cuts or rejects to my wall, sat around of an evening admiring my smart arse and polishing my cynical overview of it all. Who wants to be part of the solution when you can be part of the problem is what I say.'

'Is this some sort of rationale for being an arms trader?'

'OK. OK. I'll get back to the subject in hand, me buying art. So when Anthony Reynolds put on Billingham's first one-man show, I was down there like a shot, got my orders in before the free wine was being handed around and the peanuts munched.'

'So that's your story. You can go back to sleep now.'

'No. Not quite. Much has been written about Charles Saatchi's position within the contemporary art world, where he buys the market follows, etc. Well, I would like to take this opportunity to brag that I bought my one of the edition of five prints of Liz reclining on her sofa before Saatchi bought his. That while the hundreds of thousands of punters were trooping past Liz reclining in all her glory like Manet's Olympia at the 'Sensation' show back in 1997, there she was hanging on my living room wall, escalating in value. While in reality she was up in the West Midlands putting on the kettle again and I'm already sitting down to sup my second cup. Don't you just love it?'

'Are you quite finished?'

'No! There is something else. Christmas 1998, Paul Graham sent me a gift. It was a big print of a photo he had taken for Jimmy and me. The photo was of the brick we had made from the ashes of the money we had burnt. It looked good but what was even better was what he had wrapped it in. It was one of the reject Billingham prints. This meant I could have my cynical overview and be part of the mess at the same time. Anyone for this piece of cake I've already eaten?'

'You're a wanker Drummond.'

And on that summation of my character I fell asleep. ✖

SICNOTES

On The Duty of Civil Disobedience by Henry David Thoreau – Not sure, exactly, where I first picked it up. It could have been Delhi, or Kathmandu, or even Kabul, which in the early seventies was still accessible to the casual traveller. I was on the hippy trail, looking for some spiritual guidance, perhaps, some way out of the network of Western values I felt myself trapped in. Obviously I wasn't the only one.

The essay is a very measured piece of work, self-consciously literary in a mannered, 19th century style, it came attached as a sort of afterword to another of Thoreau's works. Very little fire or passion, rather a kind of cold, calculating, wilful, act of literary sabotage, its title makes it clear what it intends. Based on Thoreau's own personal protest against his government's continuing support for slavery, it focuses on the need for moral leverage in a world dominated by political pragmatism.

Thoreau was one of a group of American artists calling themselves the Transcendentalists, deeply influenced by Hindu culture. It's when you discover the literary provenance of the book that you begin to realise its full significance, the fact that Gandhi read it as a young barrister in South Africa, and that later, under Gandhi's influence, Nelson Mandela read it too.

Thus an obscure 19th century American writer, hardly noticed in his time, came to have an effect upon world history and the spread of political ideas. It makes you realise how powerful books can be.

C J Stone

The **SAVAGE** beast

Sic **meets prototype punk and** *England's Dreaming* **author Jon Savage**

"**D**id you see fucking Frank Skinner presenting the Brits? I'm not a violent person but I'd really like to fucking hit him!" says Jon Savage in his really posh voice. Savage is the writer and critic best known as the man who put punk rock in context in *England's Dreaming*. We're meeting up in a cafe in Manchester the day after the annual droolfest and toady-up of the Brit Awards. Kylie's arse as the new gay icon has left him cold, he's a fan of pop's "outcasts, the gay boys and the weird straights and the stroppy girls and the gay girls..." And all that's on offer are various body parts in the form of Britney's tummy, Kylie's arse and Destiny's tits. Savage is despairing of contemporary pop culture, he thinks it's too straight and going to hell in a mass-produced handcart.

"One of the most baffling and irritating things for me about contemporary culture is the redrawing of the sex and gender map of the '50s: lad culture, the rise of football, the cultural dynamic principle. What annoyed me about seeing Frank Skinner at the Brits is that he's one of the main agents of this.

"One has had to struggle to feel OK about being gay and fight against all that stuff and I can't believe it's all come back, and people expect you to play along with it. It's all part of the general political thrust, the new right was fantastically successful from 1975 onwards, not only in the sphere of economics."

Sic wanted to talk to Savage because he doesn't fit in with the ethos that everything should be product and nothing really matters. He's an enthusiast, an obsessive and a critical fan. When he's interested in something he looks underneath it for the bugs, links it to its antecedents, asks awkward questions, sees its strengths and flaws

A SHIFT IN PERSPECTIVE

"YOU HAD TO LIVE THROUGH '76 AND '77 AND IT WAS VERY EXCITING AND THEN '78 AND '79 JUST FELT LIKE CACK... AND SO YOU HAD TO START PLANNING A WAY OUT OF THAT"

JON SAVAGE

and loves or hates it nonetheless. Because he's thorough he finds the politics in pop culture, making links which explain why pop changes our lives for better or worse. For all his rants and polemic he knows the difference between being critical and cruel. At the moment he's writing a book about the Beatles but because it's Savage it will be a cultural, political and psychological history of the 20th century. And behind it all is the simple idea that he loves the band.

"All you have to do is play the music. The other day I listened to 'I am the Walrus'," says Savage, "and I thought 'How come a really major pop group made this record, it's so angry and it's so weird?' So in a way they are an inspiration because they're an example of somebody who has got everything that this society thinks that people want... and they wanted more, and that's very interesting.

"The fact that they were successful and didn't go like Elvis, they didn't go for cheeseburgers and Las Vegas. They really made an effort, a lot of the things they did were stupid, a lot of their positions were contradictory but they really made an effort to be very inquiring."

Some of Savage's positions are contradictory – like his relative ignorance but intense dislike of football – but you could never accuse him of not being inquiring. One of the main reasons we wanted to do a magazine was to ask what leads up to creative and political explosions. How could the Beatles take such massive creative leaps? Why was there more fusion between politics and pop in the '60s and then again in the '70s with punk rock than there is now?

Are creative leaps the result of collectivity or is there such a thing as individual genius? Or maybe a push forward needs the creative input of loads of different people but it takes one person to bring it together?

"In the case of punk that may well have been Johnny Rotten. I think it has to be a person bringing it together and a person can embody the age, there's timing and then there's having really good quality of input, having a lot of people around. The Stones had a lot of people around, the Beatles had a lot of people around all the time, Missy Elliot has probably got loads of people around, and it depends upon the person who physically embodies whatever this thing is not to turn into Elvis. And Elvis tried hard not to be Elvis but he still turned into Elvis, poor soul."

"**The Beatles are an inspiration because they had everything that this society thinks that people want... and they wanted more**"

"One of the ironies of pop success," wrote Savage in 1989, "is that it lends not only general recognition to the marginal but also the alienation of celebrity to the individual who embodies the many." Or to paraphrase Larkin, "Fame, it fucks you up."

Savage was fucked up by the attempt to live like a real punk and the disappointment that the first rush of punk didn't remake the world in seven days: "The initial wave of punk was very speedy, burn up, burn out and post punk it was very hard for me because I was literally burnt out. I'd taken too many drugs, written too many words and been through too much peculiar stuff in those two years. In 1978 I had a funny turn and went very strange for about three days, I was catatonic and so it became a case, to some extent, of survival."

The son of a "funny, immigrant, craftsman, bourgeois", punk's outsider ethos suited Savage's emotional make-up. He's frightened of large crowds and feels uncomfortable with pubs, football terraces and community singing – "It's not something that I was born and raised to" – but he still chases the idea of community through music. Savage's world was transformed by pop: "When I heard 'You Really Got Me' and saw Dave Davies looking like a girl I thought OK, right this is it, I've got something to manoeuvre with now, this is being sanctioned, this is pop music, this is really strange, and the noise... don't forget the noise." Punk provided an umbrella for outcasts and weirdos; dance music and the Hacienda was a utopian sound clash where taking drugs and dancing was a glimpse of what the world could be like if everybody got along.

"Then you got the Happy Mondays who I can't stand. Shaun Ryder, poison dwarf, drug freak... their influence was disastrous. The sensitive straight boys now think they have to be tough, the gay boys think they have to be nellies like Graham Norton."

As Savage said in the *Guardian* in 1994: "Since the late 1980s there has been a gradual media process through which the New Man (sensitive, pro-feminist and chore-sharing) slowly became the New Lad (he liked a night out with the boys) to the unreconstructed Lad, which is where we are today. This Lad, as many articles with Baddiel and Skinner point out, is a wilfully untidy, politically uninterested B-L-O-K-E."

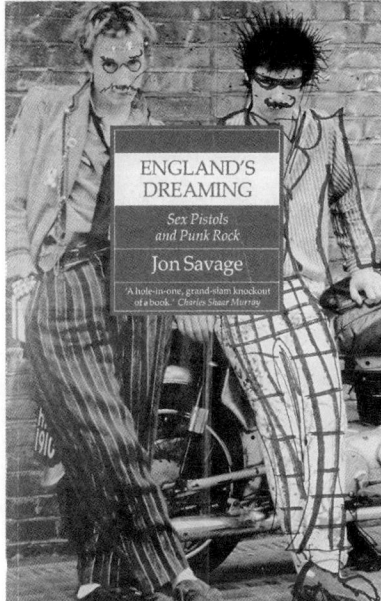

Style culture also pushed pop into more conservative territory. If the end of the seventies were a bullet train, culturally the eighties were a measured plod back into the station. "Punk rock was a shift in perspective," said Magazine's Howard Devoto in an interview with Savage in 1977. For a brief spell self-empowerment, community, creativity and political involvement were at least as important as getting on the telly. Then came the '80s and style culture with the depoliticisation of style and emphasis on the individual. Thatcher famously said "There is no society" and style culture's response was "I'm gorgeous... look at me!" Kids no longer looked like their parents but it was mostly a superficial rebellion. There were exceptions like Frankie Goes To Hollywood (who actually admitted to having sex) but Boy George neatly encapsulated style culture when he dressed up like a little girl's china doll but reassured the status quo that he was neutered when he said he'd rather have a cup of tea than sex. Style culture took the threat out of being different. Savage was involved in the early days writing for *The Face* and looks back with ambivalence:

"My viewpoint is I'd come out of the period of punk and was very disappointed with punk, which was very, very acute. You had to live through '76 and '77 and it was very exciting and then '78 and '79 just felt like cack... and so you had to start planning a way out of that, so I came into the world from the point of view of music and pop rather than politics. Fuck it, there was an element emotionally why I could understand why people said 'Fuck art... let's dance!' Don't forget there was fantastic music in that period, the music of black America.

"It's very interesting to see the process of corruption; I regard the eighties as a decade of corruption. The main thing about corruption is that you don't know that it's there, that it's working on you until it's already started working. It's insidious. In *The Face* I wrote a lot about gender issues and sexuality in pop music and the history of pop culture – which are still themes I work with – and also the politics of deception, the way that people see things and the way that people were trained to see things. So that was my agenda but from 1985 on I became more critical. I left *The Face* after Julie Burchill wrote a piece saying how wonderful Mrs Thatcher was, so I wrote a letter saying I don't want to be part of a magazine along with someone so vile, so I was out of it."

The honeymoon period of 'Fuck art... let's dance!' was well over by 1987 when Savage wrote in the *New Statesman*: "But style culture – like the definition of post-modernism that it embodied – had a fatal flaw: in its obsession with the minutiae of style, in its very aspiration it failed to develop any political or theoretical distance from wider economic and social trends. Style culture quickly became the cutting edge of Thatcherite consumerism and social mobility: its traces can now be seen in pop videos and all over Fleet Street."

Culture didn't just lose control and swerve to the right like a drunk driver. Politically the '80s are remembered for the attacks on the unions through the miners and the print workers, while youth in general was also under siege. Education – the breathing space between school and work – was narrowed down, and the benefit system, which had subsidised the creativity of punk and beyond, was squeezed into almost non-existence. The Criminal Justice Bill and the outlawing of free parties and sound systems tried to criminalise hundreds of thousands of 18–24 year olds who just wanted to have a good time. The attack on youth was an attempt to reimpose the work ethic.

"They brought in legislation against kids," says Savage, "with student loans, grants, all the stuff about kids not being able to leave home because there was a gap in the benefit system between sixteen, seventeen and eighteen... contrary to what everybody thinks now, Mrs Thatcher didn't just walk in and

> "Style culture quickly became the cutting edge of Thatcherite consumerism and social mobility: its traces can now be seen in pop videos and all over Fleet Street"

have an easy time, there were struggles right to the end of the Thatcher period and beyond."

Part of the swing towards Kylie is timing. Savage's generation grew up under the shadow of the bomb and it shaped and politicised them:

"I was thinking about this today, the nuclear bomb was the big split. I think it changed absolutely everything, our consciousness was formed by it. The bomb posed a huge existential problem such as no other generation faced: 'We might all get blown up tomorrow, what the fuck are we gonna do?'"

It took ten years from Hiroshima and Nagasaki for culture to veer off into what we think of as rock'n'roll, and as Jerry Rubin put it: "The new left sprang from Elvis's hips." So could September 11 and awareness of mortality lead to another explosion of creativity?

"The mass media has done all it can to dampen September 11 down and we have the modern equivalent of Roman Emperors and the Coliseums to distract us... that's celebrity culture. Celebrities are thrown to the lions as we watch. Celebrity culture is still obsessing everybody... unless you live in New York, people in New York are still traumatised. What the ruling class has done in the UK and Europe is to divert attention with the 'war' and try and pretend it never happened."

New York aside, there's an argument that says that instead of making Americans feel vulnerable it's made the US government feel invincible because now Bush has a mandate to do anything he wants in the name of the 'war on terrorism'.

"Somebody wrote a piece the other day saying 'Every time Americans look in the rear view mirror they see September 11'. It justifies everything. One has to hope that it's the last throw of the same

mixture of oil, big business, media, Christianity and right wingery that killed Kennedy... that killed Martin Luther King. This is the horrible strand of American life that is ruining America. It's the kind of America that puts everybody in prison shouting 'three strikes and you're out.' Whatever happened to American freedom? There's a lot of really great things about America... " Which takes us back to rock'n'roll, to the West Coast garage groups like the Zeros that Savage loves and copies CDs of because he thinks everybody ought to hear them.

I like Jon Savage. He's combative and eccentric and probably can't cook because he buys a week's worth of takeaway meals from the cafe we're in (which I can't help thinking will taste funny by Friday). Still, he's a genuinely nice man who takes trivial, throwaway pop culture very, very seriously. In an age of cultural commentators saying not much more than "I remember... clackers... the Clash... the World Cup blah blah blah..." he chases the meaning behind the word and moment: "Although I do love ephemeral stuff, in the end given that I don't have children I want to leave some lasting work." He writes about the awkward bits of pop culture, the sexual meaning between the lines, the tension between art and commerce, the gaps between myth and reality.

"Scott Fitzgerald is a great writer and he said human beings are capable of holding two contradictory ideas in their heads at the same time. I believe it's the contradictions that make things interesting and that's not a cop-out. It's very difficult to live by your principles in this society and this society throws up contradictions so much that one cannot use contradictions as a reason not to do things." ✖

Bomb culture

Mick Farren

The subtitle for the movie *Dr. Strangelove* was 'How I learned to stop worrying and love the bomb'. It served us pretty damn well back in the last millennium but, in this new one, it has become redundant. We now have to start worrying again and remember the bomb. Only a matter of a year or so ago, the general feeling was that we had made it through the Cold War intact. The Atomic Age had passed its 50th anniversary, and for more than half a century, perhaps more by luck than judgement, we had survived. Three generations have grown to maturity with the learned ability to protect their mental health by tuning out the constant background knowledge that we had the technology to ensure the extinction of this species, along with most other life on the planet. Superpower nuclear arsenals were gradually being dismantled, and an atomic kitsch was developing, as in the late night TV commercials for videotapes of nuclear explosions, that came complete with 3D glasses, like a form of morbid nuclear pornography. Before we condemn this as a sick media aberration, we have to look back and reflect how such seeming aberrations may just have been a final legacy of a popular culture that was the primary release valve for our nuclear anxieties, horrors and misconceptions, and may have actually been what saved our collective global ass.

Post-World War II mass pop culture – all the B-movie, radiation-spawned mutant lizards, and giant insects, incredible shrinking men and 50ft women, the slew of post-nuclear fantasies, both in print and film, the rock'n'roll songs and the comic books – can now be easily recognised as the tips of a massive but lifesaving cultural and psychological iceberg. One of the earliest video games, Missile Command, encouraged players to wipe out cities on the other side of the planet with first strike launches. At the same time, the flourishing atom-age folklore that told of secret installations like Mt. Weather (where the chosen few would wait out the horror in entire underground cities), or the story of the brown bear that almost triggered an accidental nuclear first strike, also provided bite-sized servings of the inherent fear that a hard rain was gonna fall. Slim Pickens riding his bomb down to the ultimate nuclear apocalypse enabled us to come to grips with the sick Freudian sexuality of nuclear weapons, and the pompous self-deception, and button-down megalomania of those who controlled their use.

This was the war that dared not speak its name, but in our cultural fantasies we could at least give it partial form, and even create a kind of mass inertia that could slow down any leadership that seemed too willing to advance to the nuclear brink

All of this may well have provided a code by which we could think about the unthinkable, and live with at least a partial idea of the unbelievable destruction that would be created by an all-out, multiple re-entry strike of fusion weapons, with ICBMs dropping from above the atmosphere like a cosmic reckoning, rendering entire continents uninhabitable, and creating a decade-long nuclear winter. This was the war that dared not speak its name, but in our cultural fantasies we could at least give it partial form, and even create a kind of mass inertia that could slow down any leadership that seemed too willing to advance to the nuclear brink.

Godzilla, Bob Dylan, Stanley Kubrick, and Mutually Assured Destruction may have helped us to survive the twentieth century, but here in the twenty first we have to very seriously look for other solutions. Even the bomb from the B52 that Slim Pickens rode whooping to Armageddon is no longer the one we have to fear. Nuclear proliferation has moved to a new and sinister phase as India and Pakistan teeter, posturing aggressively, on the brink of atomic

A RARE MOMENT
"The waning moon went zonktoosh
And quickly put itting jogtish
It was quite the most moving trundleplop of my life.
Suddenly things changed.
It was if a new tinkle titti ponk had come down from Heaven.
I am not normally a believer in snottledink
But this time things were different.
(Do you want me to go on?)"

Assuming that you do want me to go on about inspirations that have in some way changed my

life, as my poem above says, I'm not normally a believer in "snottledink" – or "ooh-ahism" as I nowadays call it. As an artist I do get ideas, lots of them – but to me these are just ideas, not inspirations. As to the kind of blinding revelation which supposedly struck St Paul on the road to Damascus, all I can say is I'm not St Paul and the road I'm on, wherever else it goes, does not lead to Damascus.

However, occasionally in my life, in an almost mystical way, quite suddenly and unexpectedly, things in an overall sense have become very clear to me. There was no

bolt from Heaven, nothing externally dramatic, no perceptible change in my lifestyle – yet from that point onwards I know I had undergone at least a slight personality shift. No drugs. I had just got high on myself.

The last such occasion was about 12 years ago after sending a photograph of my Hitler sculpture, 'Penny for Your Thoughts' to the Keeper of Art at the Imperial War Museum. This was prompted by an article in the *Guardian* about the sculptor, Bill Woodrow, who was having an exhibition there. To my amazement the Museum got back to me (in two confrontation. We now look at multiple scenarios of small messy nuclear exchanges, and their potentially frightening human and environmental impact. We can anticipate the battlefield incidents and the incineration of huge, overcrowded cities. Maybe most frightening of all is the fact that the majority of these newly emergent nuclear powers don't share the imprecise but effective nuke culture that helped save us in the West.

This was confirmed by the Indian novelist Arundhati Roy in an article recently published in the *Nation*. "'Why isn't there a peace movement?' Western journalists ask me ingenuously. How can there be a peace movement when, for most people in India, peace means a daily battle: for food, for water, for shelter, for dignity? War, on the other hand, is something professional soldiers fight far away on the border. And nuclear war, well, that's completely outside of the realm of most people's comprehension. No-one knows what a nuclear bomb is. No-one cares to explain."

On a purely military level, the current situation in Kashmir is dangerously reminiscent of the Iron Curtain stand-off on the frontier between East and West Germany in the 1950s and 60s. The Indians have a significant superiority on the ground, and if, as they used to say in our own Cold War, 'the balloon goes up', the odds are that any India advance would easily roll over the Pakistani positions. In any tactical scenario that finds Pakistani conventional forces in full retreat, the temptation for that country's generals, who also wield overwhelming political power, will be to resort to battlefield nuclear weapons. And once the first mushroom cloud rises from the hills of Kashmir, the genie is out of the bottle. The Indian response could easily be to incinerate a small Pakistani city, and from there it can only escalate to Calcutta and Karachi. As both JFK and Bertrand Russell pointed out in their individual ways, once war is cut loose, it inevitably takes on a life of its own, and, to make matters even more dangerously complicated, this would be an atomic border war between countries in such close geographic proximity that no early warning or 'hot line' breathing space for negotiation is possible.

days) and stated an interest in buying the piece – which they eventually did; but at that stage I, as an unknown artist, was naturally very excited.

Shortly afterwards I went to a theatre, where my son was performing in a dance choreographed by an Israeli woman, followed by some Israeli dances. During the dances it became blindingly clear to me that my sculpture could not have been made by anyone other than a Jewish artist. There was no utterly logical, conclusive justification for this view – I just knew. I'm not a particularly 'Jewish' Jew. I don't attend synagogue, my wife isn't Jewish and I abhor Sharon's behaviour towards the Palestinians; yet I've always admitted to being Jewish and am proud of my Jewish heritage. I had for many years realised that in one's work as an artist one must strive to be true to one's inner self. I suppose I felt then I had got there; also the flavour of life to me from that point onwards changed. In the words of my poem "...this time things were different."

Richard Niman

Not that either India or Pakistan seem to be thinking in terms of hot lines or one-minute-to-midnight diplomacy. As one old English NATO general said on TV the other night (no, I'm afraid I didn't catch his name), "Even the military hierarchies don't really understand the power of nuclear weapons. They think they're lobbing a big hand grenade." Snobbish, superior, and probably racist, but, as confirmed by Arundhati Roy, lethally true. The prevailing attitude would seem to be that of General Mirza Aslam Beg: "We can take a first strike, a second, or even a third. You can die crossing the street, or you can die in a nuclear war." Further insight came from Pervez Hoodbhoy writing in the *Los Angeles Times*. "Nuclear ignorance is almost total, extending even to the educated. Some students at the University of Islamabad where I teach said, when asked, that a nuclear war would be the end of the world. Others thought of nukes as just bigger bombs. Many said it was not their concern but the army's. Almost no-one knew about the possibility of a nuclear firestorm, about residual radioactivity or damage to the gene pool… for the masses, (nuclear weapons) are symbols of national glory."

These attitudes are being formed against a background devoid of the horror movies, the comic book heroes, the science fiction, and the grass roots myth and rumour, rock'n'roll lyrics, the work of the beat generation, the hippies, and punks who followed, as they both shaped and reflected the first nuclear half century. The Indians and Pakistanis have no shared memory of a Cuban Missile Crisis when we in the West almost ran out of road. With a highly controlled media – especially TV – they have yet to even face the 1950s absurdity of civil defence drills, fallout shelters, *Duck & Cover*, and the idea that you could hide from an atomic attack behind a briefcase, or under a desk; or the bizarre jargon that was employed to discuss the unthinkable, and the horrifying in-fighting over who actually controlled the weapons and extent of their manufacture. Sanity was a hard enough fight in the West. When film-makers attempted to portray a post-nuke wasteland as it really might be, the protests and accusations flew. In the early 1960s, British director Peter Watkins made *The War Game* for the BBC, who immediately banned it as "too depressing". Twenty years later, in the US, ABC produced *The Day After* as a Sunday night made-for-TV movie, and although the show wasn't banned, the producers were accused by the Reagan administration and its media supporters of everything from defeatism to out-and-out treason. The irony was that both films freely admitted that they deliberately understated the scope of the devastation. The new generation of emergent atomic powers have yet to state anything or so much as approach that phase of debate.

So can anything be done? In two words: probably not. Even if we could send care packages of *Godzilla, Dr. Strangelove*, and CND, they would be rejected, and maybe rightly so, as cultural imperialism. Intervention by world leaders? I wouldn't trust George W. to go out for a beer and pork pies and get it right. For once, we in the West will be the lone voices crying in the wilderness. The only hope I can extend is that, back in 1962, when it looked as though apocalyptic annihilation was only a day away, the lone voices cried loud and long. And you know what? It fucking worked! Crying, waiting and hoping, to paraphrase Buddy Holly, may be the only options open to us, so let's cry real loud. ✱

OK!

FIRST FOR LEFTIST GOSSIP

ISSUE 328•MAY 1 2002•£1.95 WEEKLY

"NEITHER SOLDIERS NOR TERRORISTS"
PROTO-CHOMSKYIST
BRITNEY

DISCUSSES POST 9/11 GLOBALISATION

JUSTIN TIMBERLAKE EXCLUSIVE

"THE REAL ENEMY IS IDEOLOGICAL ZEALOTRY FUELLED BY INDUSTRIALISATION"

REVEALED! THE LANGUAGE OF EMANCIPATORY POLITICS AND MY NIGHT OF PASSIONATE DISCOURSE WITH JASON FROM BLUE!

WHAT BEN AFFLECK *REALLY* THINKS ABOUT BOOKCHIN'S VIEW OF BOURGEOIS SOCIOLOGY

ARE YOU A FLIRT WHO LOVES INCLUSIVE DEMOCRACY? FIND OUT IN OUR SPECIAL DIALECTICAL QUIZ!

KATE

THE INHERENT RECUPERATION OF THE RADICAL MILIEU - BY THAT WOMAN WHO WON BIG BROTHER

"I've waited my whole life to see this"

Caroline Coon, artist, writer and veteran of both the hippy movement and punk, walks and talks Sic *through a whistle-stop and random tour of a century of art, at the exhibition* Paris, Capital of the Arts 1900–1968

Suzanne Valadon, *The Fortune Teller*, 1912

Suzanne Valadon
The Fortune Teller, 1912
Caroline Coon sashays into the first gallery and stops dead.

"I've wanted to see this painting almost all my life. It's incredible that through the work of feminist politics/feminist discussion over the last 20 years, paintings like this are now being introduced into the main narrative."

She pauses and turns to me.

"So who do you think painted it?"

I'm ten years old again grasping for an answer.

"A... a... woman?"

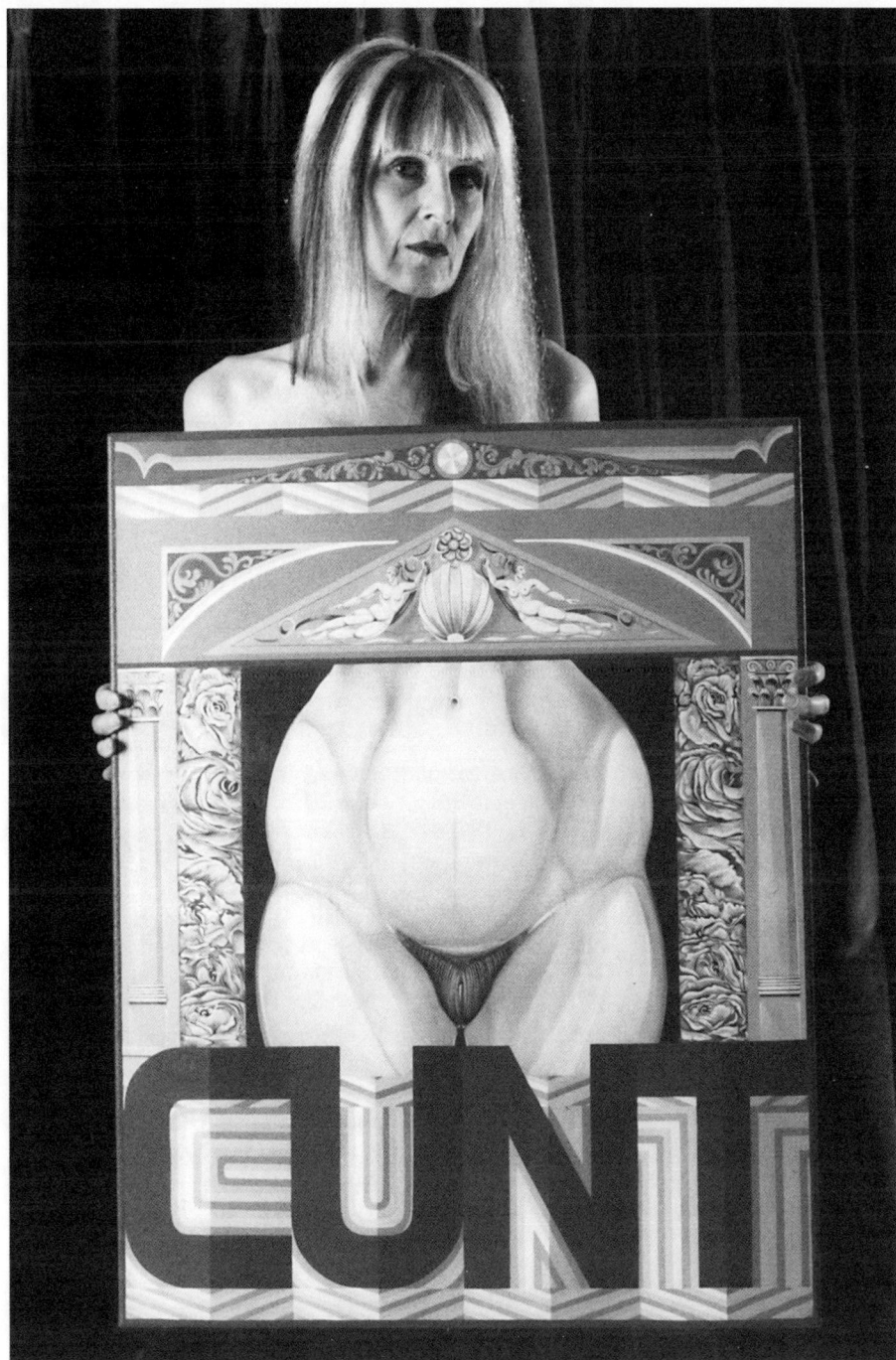

I've been saved by the word 'feminist' in her lead-up.

"Why?"

Oh Christ.

"I think it's by a woman because... because... because there's obviously a relationship going on between them and they're not just passive."

"OK," says Caroline, pleased that I'm trying to keep up. "On the whole one is so used to *not* seeing women's art in these great academies. It's by an artist called Suzanne Valadon, and she to me is one of the most important artists of the era. She was known a lot through being painted by other artists, she was an inspiration for other painters. She was very much an artist's model but she was very much a great painter herself. Because she was a working class woman, the illegitimate daughter of a washer-woman who came from the countryside of Paris, for her to break through and do an incredible painting like this... she's painting nudes, which for women was very dangerous. She's painting her female contemporaries who are middle class women who were absolutely prevented from making this kind of work. They had to be ladylike, those middle-class women; they had to paint domestic scenes.

"She knows what it's like to pose nude. Women like Suzanne Valadon, like Eva Gonzalez who's also a painter, they were working class, therefore they had to model to earn their living. They were all considered prostitutes; to model was to be a prostitute. You could look at her as painted by a Picasso or Manet – Manet was a big friend of hers. Because she was

> **"These women who wore trousers – at a time when it was illegal to dress as a man – these women were kicking over the traces saying 'I want to live'..."**

working class she had access to liberation."

"You mean she wasn't expected to be a lady," I say ingenuously.

"She could hang out in the pubs and get drunk *but* she was written out of the narrative of art history. Very recently a French art critic said 'of course she was just a whore!' She painted male nudes too. I'm crying because I've only ever seen this illustrated in a small book which I had to get from the library in black and white. I can't believe that you spotted it was done by a woman but in a way it should stand on its own.

"She had a reputation for being just as drunk as the men, she had affairs. The way she lived was brave, courageous an absolute political statement and caused her no end of problems; whereas all the men who behaved like that were validated and valorised.

"When she was a young woman she sold quite a bit of her painting but the moment she became old she just couldn't sell. Whereas a man as he gets older, his paintings get more heroic, he's viewed as a wonderful old lion. For her, the older she was, the more difficult she found it to sell paintings."

Tamara de Lempicka

portrait of La Duchesse de la Salle, 1925

"Tamara de Lempicka who to me was *just* staggering. The Duchess... isn't it unbelievable what she's painting there..."

Me: "1925... If she turned up dressed like that... people would have a thrombosis"

"Listen... these women who dressed

Tamara de Lempicka, *portrait of La Duchesse de la Salle*, 1925

like this, and it was illegal in Paris at this time to dress as a man, these women were kicking over the traces saying 'I want to live, I want my place in the workplace.' They were wearing trousers and it was absolutely sensational. Now this kind of looks like a style statement in a way, then it was radical and revolutionary."

Me: "Things always get co-opted into a style statement."

"Tempicka was fascinating because she was a Russian aristocrat," says Caroline, warming to her theme. "All her land and stuff was taken away by the revolution so she escapes to Paris, paints this incredible, highly polished art deco work, wonderful nude men... fantastic nude men, fantastic nude women all highly stylised. And she used to wear furs... very reminiscent of Hollywood.

Me: "She's a bit Joan Crawford."

"She's a bit Joan Crawford but more elegant because Joan Crawford is mimicking wealth and she is *it*. She's dripping in it, she has that real aristocratic style, the pearls, the silks, the fantastic Mercedes. She drives a car, her auto-portrait at this time, her self-portrait is her at the wheel of a car but of course it's unusual to see her included here because she was considered too vulgar and she was *just* a woman. It's great to see her lined up at last with what's considered to be the masters of European art."

I point at a Picasso: "That is a fantastic classical portrait but the Tempicka has so much more life."

"That's a fantastic portrait. This is why I think Picasso can do abstract art later on because he's done that journey from this kind of work. I'm glad you like Tempicka, I relish her. She was an aristocrat but because she had lost all her money she had to earn a living. She earned a fortune from Hollywood – Joan Crawford might have had a Tamara de Tempicka painting, so those were the people who bought her work. Establishment art critics would say that her work was vulgar."

Me: "Vulgarity in a woman, at that time, would be a sign that she was stepping outside the law."

"I don't see vulgarity as a pejorative, I think vulgarity is something to be relished. It's having a good time, it's fucking and liking good music, drinking and coming. Ladies weren't allowed to be vulgar, you couldn't be vulgar... women who wanted to be accepted into society spent their whole lives not being vulgar. Whereas the men could be vulgar in the brothel, women didn't have that choice.

Me: "There's a flood of women out of Russia straight after the revolution, creatively firing on all cylinders."

Romaine Brooks

Jean Cocteau in the Era of the Big Wheel 1912

"Portrait of Jean Cocteau... by Romaine Brooks. She was one of the out, gay women of the era who got arrested with Colette for dressing up as men. They were making statements, they wore suits and sashayed down the Champs Elysées smoking cigarettes and being out as women dressed as men. It caused a huge scandal. Because it was so scandalous to see women parading around in trousers they passed a law to ban it. So she was painting Jean Cocteau who was also scandalised because he was out gay. Which was illegal."

Me: "What's so great about that is it's called 'in the era of the big wheel' so you get the idea that this is a world that's turning. We're used to technology now but then it was a source of hope."

Romaine Brooks, *Jean Cocteau in the Era of the Big Wheel*, 1912

Francis Picabia

Adoration of the Calf, 1941–42

Caroline and I are wandering round the room which deals with the rise of fascism, the French occupation, collaboration and the post-war problem of coming to terms with it all. I'm glad that the paintings are sombre, darker than the turn of the century optimism. There'd be something obscene about too much jollity.

"Here is the fact that Europe has been through this incredibly brutal experience," says Caroline.

There's been a Picabia in almost every room in the gallery; as Paris changed, so did he – always moving, experimenting. Caroline tells me that he wasn't particularly left wing.

"Picabia wasn't on the left and yet he could still stand outside fascism and paint that." I'm surprised.

"Do you get Salvador Dali?" I ask for no other reason than the Adoration of the Calf has a point and says something direct, whereas Dali always seems to be trying to hard to be clever and weird, an elaborate confidence trick.

"Yes, if I had to name five paintings in the world I wouldn't go to Dali but what he did with his life as an artist was riveting. I'd question his politics but the whole idea of making yourself into the spectacle."

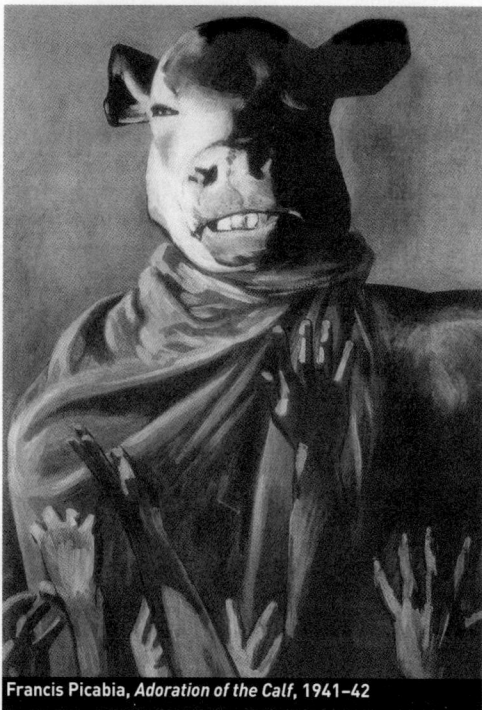

Francis Picabia, *Adoration of the Calf*, 1941–42

Jean Dubuffett

The Villager with Close-Cropped Hair, 1947 Building Facades from Mirobolus, 1946

Jean Dubuffett, *Building Facades from Mirobolus*, 1946

"I like how dark it is," I say pointing at *The Villager* and its neighbour *Building Facades*: "There's a thing here saying that these buildings may have contained collaborationist deals, Nazis billeted and Jewish

Jean Dubuffett, *The Villager with Close-Cropped Hair, 1947*

families deported. For me that works much better than 'The Horrors of War' thing. It's like 'war is here' and people are protesting quietly because it's all you can do."

"Given the way that an artist could handle it, that's an incredible piece."

Antonin Artaud, *Self-Portrait, 1947*

Antonin Artaud

Self-Portrait, 1947

"Antonin Artaud... self-portrait. His drawings are just brilliant. He was a brilliant writer, surrealist, thinker, revolutionary who was so brilliant that he kept being tipped into madness. All the time he was off the edge he was painting and drawing.

"This is what we would call the first decade of the modern era... abstract expressionism... think what the Americans are beginning to do. What these European paintings are taking to America."

Jean Fautrier

Large Tragic Head, 1942

"Fautrier abstract works," says Caroline excited by a whole section of Fautrier. "After he died his wife began naming them. He's another one of the drunk, distressed artists slipping into mental hospitals. Like Artaud, Fautrier was part of this group who were living in extreme emotion almost into madness but externalising this extreme of emotion and despair onto paper. This was the period when the great hope to save culture was the idea of communism, one is beginning to realise that it's not going to happen. What's happening in Russia is this sense of despair, betrayal,

Jean Fautrier, *Large Tragic Head*, 1942

disillusionment with the idea that state communism could make life worthwhile for working people... and make for a better world. People are beginning to realise that it's not going to happen."

Henri Michaux

Mescaline Pictures

"Michaux was the one I knew about in the sixties. People who were the avatars of acid talked about him. As the idea that drugs were taking a hold in the sixties I did think about 'Can I work round drugs?' Given also the myth of the artist who was always drunk and stuff – and I

Advertisement

say 'myth'. So hearing of Michaux doing drawings under the influence of mescaline, I did a trip and tried to paint. Actually, acid completely destroyed me and I could hardly function. But his works, we've only got two here, are incredible pictures and it's debatable whether he could have done it without. So he's washing his paper with water colours of pinks and blues and letting his hand just kind of wander. You get this explosion of emotion.

Henri Michaux, *Mescaline Pictures*

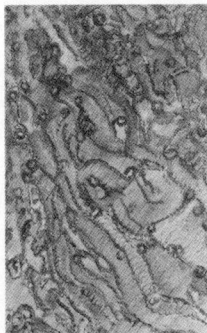
Henri Michaux, *Mescaline Pictures*

"I'm very interested in this idea that you have to be stoned or out of your mind, or drunk to paint. Actually you don't, but quite a few artists have experimented."

"I bet you can work like that," I say "but you also need the discipline to get up in the morning and do it again. To carry on and improve and push yourself."

"Michaux was outside the art world because he was always too poor to have exhibitions. In his lifetime he didn't really have exhibitions, it's only after his deaths that these works done in grimy bedsits come to life.

"It's interesting to compare European abstract art and American. The Americans had much more space. European art, the size of it, is essentially what you can get into your studio... in a normal house size room. The huge paintings which Pollock was doing could only be done in a country as big as Russia or America. Except you weren't allowed to paint abstracts in Russia."

"Russia is huge in geographical terms but in mental space it's much smaller," I say. "But also it's to do with the American dream, with the idea that you can expand, and expand and expand. And people weren't disillusioned with the American dream in the '50s, it hadn't been disproved and people believed in it in a way that they don't anymore. But maybe that's just a cliché, it depends what your circumstances are as to whether or not you have or had faith in the American dream."

Caroline shakes her head amazed: "It's bizarre but America is still the place where refugees and all oppressed peoples head for. As dreadful and dire as America has turned out to be in the last 30 years, it's the worst that humans can be, and given that we want the kind of optimistic life that we want, we go to the US and see what the right wing have done to it and think how terrible it is; on the other hand if you were living in South Korea or Afghanistan it's paradise."

Me: "Like economic refuges coming here. Sivanandan says that economic refugees are political refugees, he's dead right."

"The most heroic thing you can do is smuggle refugees into this country," says Caroline making the gallery attendant turn round and look. "I always feel that I should do it. The poor lorry drivers who are getting fined £3,000, it's a very heroic thing to do."

Yves Klein
*Untitled
Anthropometry
(ANT 101) 1960*
"Yves Klein," says
Caroline with
venom. She stops
before a massive
blue and gold
abstract which
almost takes up a
wall. "As a young
student I
absolutely loathed
him. He's about
the 1960s. How
do you think that
painting is made?"

I've never
heard of Yves
Klein but I did see
Big Brother when

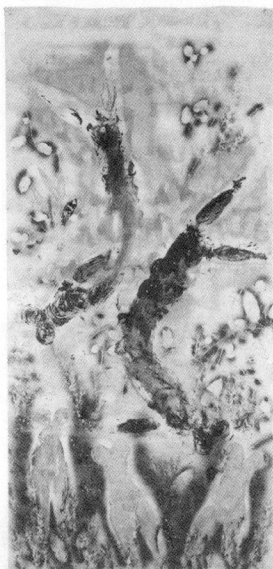

Yves Klein, *Untitled
Anthropometry (ANT 101)*, 1960

they painted their bodies and pressed
themselves against walls. I can recognise
breast imprints when I see them: "Is it a
woman's body covered in paint and she
has to lie on the canvas?"

"Right. Actually politics is here...
given the way that he's using a woman's
body as a paintbrush, as an object, given
the way that those men actually treated
women and were having working class
liberation, male sexual liberation but the

"Politics is here... given the way that he's using a woman's body as a paintbrush, as an object, given the way that those men were having working class liberation, male sexual liberation but the place of women in culture was viciously repressed"

place of women in culture was viciously
repressed. And this man was absolutely
championed for having nude models.
Now I can look at it a bit more
generously."

Me: "She has enormous breasts."

"It's not that good, Making the
painting was an event, titillation because
these nude women were there."

Me: "It's like two crayfish fighting."

"Takes a lot of space, that's a very
political piece, we're getting into what
the sixties were about, what these men
didn't want anything to do with... gender
and race."

Me: "Whereas other people saw the
failure of state communism and
capitalism as an opening for something
else these men just saw themselves."

"A lot of looking at abstract stuff, new
materials, we're getting plastic... it's not
political."

Me: "Except that reclaiming of space
and creativity is intensely political
because it's always a struggle between
capital and human nature and desire."

"I look at this work with gritted teeth
because of what my role was in culture at
that time. These men have got the space
and the indulgence to be able to emerge
themselves in this area of painting
pleasure whereas for me abortion was

illegal, I wasn't allowed to be educated, to be an artist was out... to be a woman was intrinsically second rate."

Me: "It's like the Jimmy Porter character in *Look Back In Anger*, you're meant to see him as angry, frustrated, seeking liberation... but he's slapping his girlfriend about as she's ironing."

"The fact that men have the space to concentrate on painting for pure pleasure when women couldn't even get out of the house, were beaten and raped. These men turned off and said it was the end of the struggle when there was plenty going on, we have to make a critique of that. Who were the male avatars of this time, people like Ken Tynan who treated women appallingly. I have to be generous to look at this work because of what these men actually stood for."

Gillies Ailaud, Eduardo Arroyo and Antonio Recalcati

To Live or Let Die, or The Tragic End of Marcel Duchamp, 1965

"The assassination of Marcel Duchamp, the idea that Readymades are killing paint so they kill Duchamp in paint. This is in a way part of what he was provoking. I think Duchamp would have appreciated this."

Me: "Assassination... is like a pulp fiction novel or a story board for a film. Starts off with Duchamp's piece... I like how cool the assassins look when they consciously make him look old and knackered.. look, one of them is having a fag while they're slapping him around, that's how cool he is."

"To me nothing works better than seeing what a person can produce in paint. But also what's missing from this is what was produced next. We see something of it in Niki de Saint Phalle's work but there's a period where women come into their own and truly take on the status quo." ✖

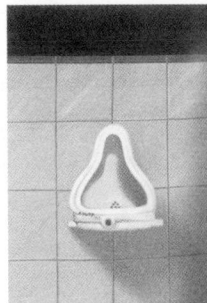

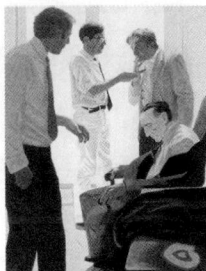

A. Gillies Ailaud, Eduardo Arroyo and Antonio Recalcati, *To Live or Let Die, or The Tragic End of Marcel Duchamp*, 1965

SUICIDE BOMBERS

**"I'm telling you my dear
that it can't happen here..."**

— *Frank Zappa*

 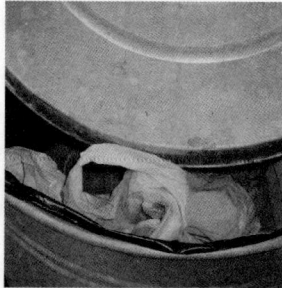 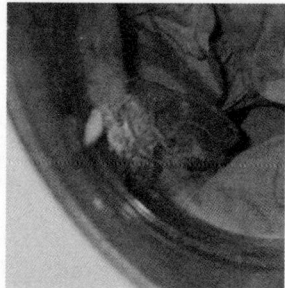

 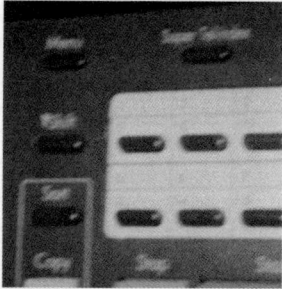 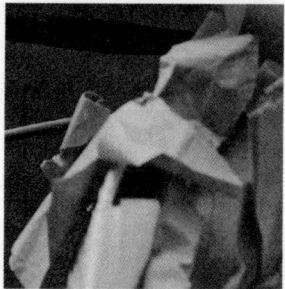

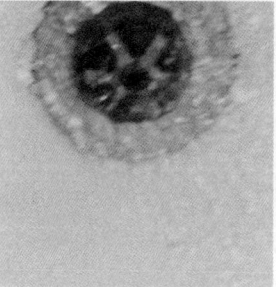  

...why not?

"I love that stuff!"

Sic **treks around pop culture with Alabama 3's**
Reverend D Wayne Love (aka Jake)

Jake Black and I are knocking on Edwyn Collins' studio door and no-one is answering. Jake has set it up for *Sic* to interview Edwyn Collins – or rather for me to tape Jake and Edwyn talking about radical pop culture – only Edwyn has obviously changed his mind. In the few years I've known Jake from Alabama 3 I've come to realise that Jake knows everything and everybody: he's the living embodiment of the six degrees phenomenon – he has links everywhere and he's liked everywhere he goes. I've watched him work a room and it's the opposite of networking: in a room full of popstars he'd befriend the cleaner. While the band are boring each other witless Jake and his new friend would be talking about Wittgenstein, Coltrane or the last scene in *The Sweet Smell of Success*. Jake drops names, but not just famous ones; he's as likely to tell you who he sat next to at

school, who first played him Solomon Burke records and who his Dad worked with as he is to mention that last week he went to dinner with Winona Ryder or that William Burroughs was his long-time pen pal. It's not who you are but what you have to say that interests Jake. So when Jake says that Edwyn Collins is Mr Pop Culture I trust his judgement.

"Hey Grace, we're at the studio now," says Jake to Edwyn Collins' girlfriend. I can't hear the other side of the conversation but it's not going well.

"You left a message? When?"

"20 minutes ago we were on the tube."

"How long?"

"What, all day?"

Jake stuffs his mobile back into his trouser pocket, and uses two hands to push his hair behind his ears.

"Whadya wanna do, Al? Grace says she rang and cancelled."

Truth is, I don't mind missing the chat with Edwyn Collins: I'd have been happy to buy him and Jake drinks and see where it went but it's Jake we really want to include in *Sic*. When he's in Alabama 3 mode as the Reverend D Wayne Love, he's dark, twisted and feeds on the power that he has over the audience. His character is seductive and demonic. It's satire mixed with break beats, blues, country & western and blue grass and it's all done with genuine love of the music – most people have heard Alabama 3's sublime 'Woke Up This Morning' theme tune for *The Sopranos*. The band's other front man is the bluesy-voiced Larry Love. His shades-at-3am world-weary slouch is the perfect foil for the Reverend's hell-and-high-water preaching. An ex-Mormon from the Welsh valleys, Larry Love well understands the power of old style religion; Alabama 3 use all its tricks but not in the service of the Lord.

The son of an old school Glasgow communist, Jake's background is working class and anti-religious:

"When I was a nipper we had this football team and the Priest came up talking to us and I remember him saying 'God's all-knowing and can see everything we do.'

"So I says: 'Can he see my Da in his Rolls Royce?'

"And the Priest goes: 'Yes, he can see your father in his Rolls Royce, the Lord sees everything.'

"And I says: 'You fucking liar, my Da hasn't got a Rolls Royce.'

"So I goes home and tells my Da this and my Da's like: 'That's my boy! I'm proud of you, son.' My father hated religion."

At 17 Jake won a prestigious Scottish poetry award and then punk rock came along with a different kind of poetry. So I ask him about punk rock and he pushes his hair behind his ears to punctuate the start of the story.

"It was the best time ever. In Glasgow there used to be this record shop called Listen on Redfield Street, and I went in there one day with my pal Victor Payne just on our lunch break from work, and they had the Sex Pistols on video doing 'Anarchy in the UK'. I'll never forget it, I was wearing this red Simon shirt and Victor just grabbed me and ripped the arm off it. And then I grabbed his arm and ripped his, and so we walked out the shop and went in RS McColls and Victor bought a big strip of fabric Elastoplast and we fastened our clothes together with that. When I went back to work after lunch I was like: 'I'm a punk rocker now!'

"And everyone was going: 'Look at your long hair, you're a couple of hippies!'

"So we decided to go to the barbers. Then we smoked a joint and thought

SICNOTES

Crass introduced me to cheap records, anarchy symbols, angry words – and the concept of DIY. If you think something is shit, don't just sit there and moan about it, get off your arse and do something about it! Without having to read all those long boring anarchist texts they made me understand – maybe not on an incredible intellectual level – but a gut feeling what anarchy meant. They made me realise that if you got together with people you could make a difference. So in Slough we wrote fanzines, made music, put on benefit gigs, jumble sales, gave free veggie food outside the local McDonalds, wrote letters to the papers, got involved in the local residents group, tried to stop planning applications and in 1984 offered support to striking miners. Anarchists who said work was shit supporting trade unionists' right to work? Crass helped me see the bigger picture. OK, so I might have been a self-righteous teetotal humourless vegan police bore at the time, but Crass taught me to forget the differences and join with others in fighting for a better world.

Warren Schnews

'punks don't go the barbers' so we got big scissors and cut big lumps in each other's hair.

"Some people have the view that punk rock was just a small coterie of art students but when it went out to the regions it became something else. It was more important in the regions because London is just a constant merry-go-round of new fashions."

We move on to Crass arriving on the scene announcing that punk had betrayed its original ideals.

"So we wrote to Crass and they said we'd like to come and play with you so we hooked up with an old hippy pal of ours, Roy Wilson, and managed to book Bearsden Borough hall. Now Bearsden is the stockbroker belt of Glasgow and 800 to 1000 punk rockers descended on Bearsden one Saturday afternoon. It was Crass and Poison Girls and it was brilliant, the place got wrecked. It was a benefit for CND but they didn't get any money because the punk rockers smashed all the toilets up. But we were a bit disappointed with Crass because they were all deadly serious, we bought them all a drink and they were like 'Oh we just want a pot of tea'. They were all twice as old as us."

Few artists cite Crass as a major influence now but they were an influence on a whole generation of artists and activists. The appeal wasn't just musical, it was the united front they presented, the notion of living and working collectively and the way they stretched being a band to include doing your own artwork, making films and writing pamphlets. What they said in the pamphlets wasn't as important as the fact that they produced them, and because they were done by designer Gee Vaucher they always looked thought-provoking and beautiful. Crass's major strength was that they were a good

> "The DIY thing was what made me realise I could be in a group if I wanted to... and a group that didn't even play music, that just made a lot of noise. If you wanted to play with us you couldn't play your own instrument, so if you played the guitar you had to play the drums"

example of people having the social and creative lives they wanted in the 'here and now'. Jake was one of the kids motivated by the DIY sensibility.

"The DIY thing was what made me realise I could be in a group if I wanted to... and a group that didn't even play music, that just made a lot of noise. Me and my pal Johnny Park had all these situationist ideas. If you wanted to play with us you couldn't play your own instrument, so if you played the guitar you had to play the drums. It was all in the spirit of scowling on musicians because it was all non-musicians, just whacking cab doors and all that... what was later called industrial music by Genesis P Orridge."

Crass were extraordinary because they refused to stay in the safe confines of rock'n'roll. They were black-clad revolutionaries who made concept albums. Serious politicos who parodied pop culture, Crass have been largely left out of the history of pop culture but those of us who lived through the few years that Crass were around took them very, very seriously. They were contradictory, inspiring and infuriating but never dull.

"I spent a year and a half analysing

Crass, I ended up going to their house and I met them and now I think they were extremely conservative in their politics. Gerry was saying the most ridiculous things and I was just a kid so they were things I didn't have arguments against then. I remember him saying: 'Capitalism doesn't necessarily have to be corrupt.'

"I said, 'I don't understand that, you'll have to explain that.'

"And his explanation was a complete load of bunk. He was talking about the kind of grass roots economy that they were trying to operate, and he was talking about pockets of radicalism within capitalism. I was coming from another place where as long as the boss held the means of production people were never going to have good political health, so I couldn't understand why he was saying that capital didn't have to be corrupt."

In the Crass years the state paid people like us to make music and print pamphlets. When capital decided to recompose itself at the end of the seventies it had to go through a transition. To get us to work for less money and with less rights it made jobs scarcer; as unemployment rose we were cushioned for a while by the dole but it was a stop-gap: once we'd become accustomed to the new economic realities they pulled the safety net – the theory was that by then we'd be too demoralised to put up a fight. But for a while the dole paid for our creative lives and the state left us alone to get on with them. Jake was a dole artist and recognises how much more difficult it is to have a creative life today.

"The dole space has closed down, the only way that kids can reinvent themselves now is through this kind of pop idol schtick, this competition thing. It's now prefab groups, groups that come through management and have

absolutely nothing to do with the way they look or sing. They don't have the dole or the artistic space to develop anymore. By giving you a wee bit of money to live on, especially if you lived with your Ma, the dole let people transform themselves. But that's gone now."

Closing up creative space is part of the depoliticisation of youth. But only one part. Anybody making political statements is now tagged as a boring, worthy oddity. Alabama 3's strategy for blowing the political stereotype includes publicly embracing hedonism, though Jake is actually ambivalent about the influence of drug culture on creativity.

"The pros are the nanoseconds of inspiration through expanded consciousness, the cons are habituating and becoming a druggy bore and the work suffering but they go hand in hand and they always will. When we first came out with all that 'straight outta rehab' stuff it was a direct reaction to all these church-going types saying: 'You can't say that, it's your duty to be clean living.' Pop culture has always been tied up with drug culture... it's embodied in Louis Armstrong."

"This is shit, man," says Jake frowning at his coffee. "What's yours like, Al?"

"Mine's shit too... do you think it's important for music to have a context?"

Jake pushes his hair behind his ears and sets off again.

"The actual process of listening means everything is reinterpreted. I could be listening to a piece of music for years and when I meet the people they tell me what was in their heads making the music and it's completely different. A good example of that is 'Woke up This Morning' – you see Tony Soprano in the titles and it's perfect but that song is about Sara Thornton killing her abusive husband. That's partly what's great about music, that it's recontextualised every time, that you can turn things backwards and you can't really do that in text, you end up talking a load of nonsense."

I ask him why he thinks black music brought pop and politics into the mainstream in the sixties and seventies and he nods.

"I love the stuff that Sly Stone, Curtis Mayfield and Sam Cooke did and it wasn't isolationist or exclusive. It got you on a musical level but it also has a context, especially the stuff that people like Marvin Gaye were doing in the early seventies just when the Vietnam way was getting really bad, it was outraging people who had never been motivated to be involved in politics before.

"Marvin Gaye went from being the Motown good boy and you would never expect him to come out with any kind of statement. But his brother came back from Vietnam and he saw the state of his brother and saw what was going on round him – it was destroying the country that war, people felt they had to do something about it. I've been reading that biography of him and he said just before he died that he was in a position where he couldn't really sing about anything else when he was doing *What's Going On*, he had to follow the dictates of his heart. He was never politically motivated so for people like that to make a whole LP a statement, things must have been pretty bad. As far as he was concerned the whole world was being turned upside down."

> "That's what's great about music, it's recontextualised every time – you can turn things backwards and you can't really do that in text, you end up talking a load of nonsense"

Maybe that's what separates Alabama 3 from other groups, they follow the dictates of their heart and they have have a huge musical and ideological storeroom to draw from. While Britain was hopping around to a drum machine and using too much hairspray in the eighties, Jake was immersing himself in jazz and orchestral music.

"I didn't listen to much pop music in the eighties. I got hold of Parker and Coltrane and started reading the biographies and it was just a complete new world so it took me about ten years to absorb it. Coltrane is as revolutionary in his own way as Parker. Coltrane was a man of incredible feeling, there's one particular track, 'Alabama', on an album called *Live at Birdland*. It's about the church bombing in Alabama where all the kids died, Coltrane happened to be in Alabama at that time and Dr King was there too, so he went along to hear King speak about the bombing, and what he did was take the whole speech home in his head and he wrote the melodic line of this piece around the rhythmic inflections of what King was saying.

"There's things Parker was doing that totally confounded people. When they heard him and Dizzy Gillespie playing together, music critics said it just sounded like a lot of noise. Music critics were just getting their heads round the chords of 'I Got Rhythm', when Parker comes out with this completely new conception."

Throughout this interview I've talked in terms of 'black' music but it's a shorthand that doesn't tell the whole story. Both Marvin Gaye and Sam Cooke are classed as archetypal soul singers but the bands they worked with in Booker T and the MG's, the floating Stax band and the Muscle Shoals musicians who played on Atlantic sessions were all integrated... and this was a point in American history when black musicians still had to enter venues through the backdoor and eat in back rooms and alleys.

"So..." I say, "I was looking at a black music website and it said that blues/jazz lost its soul when it entered the mainstream and was embraced by a white audience."

Jake looks horrified, like a stunned Wild Bill Hickok he's momentarily lost for words. He puts his fork down, eyes me seriously and asks:

"How can the articulation of feeling through playing music be the exclusive province of a particular race? All it does is engenders racism."

Jake waits for a counter-argument but

I haven't got one. Instead I change tack and ask him why artists rarely make political statements anymore.

"Making political statements, especially for musicians, is now seen as totally uncool. And if you do make a political statement how is it going to be disseminated? Where are people going to pick it up? Are they going to pick it up in the so-called qualities and the so-called pop papers which are more or less just promo mags now? Basically an editor sits there with loads of press kits from record companies, he picks the most interesting one that he's going to get the best junket out of. So they send some hack out and you're going to have to treat them nice for five days... business class blahdee, blahdee, blah, blah. All these things are is promotional magazines for companies that are putting the most money in their pockets. It's complete payola but they've managed to cut out all the illegalities. So if you want to make any kind of political statement now it's

SICNOTES

When I was about 15 I went to see the school play, I suppose for the usual reasons that a) it might be a laugh and b) some of my mates were in it, so lots of opportunity to take the piss should they fuck it up. The play was *Caucasian Chalk Circle* by Bertolt Brecht. To be fair the performances were great considering it was a school play but the writing turned my head for ever. I had never realised that a play could be so political and yet so much fun. It is the tale of a child who is abandoned by her aristocratic family and looked after by the nanny/maid. She takes the child on a series of adventures and travels and eventually meets up with the child's real mum, who demands the child

back. A Solomon-type judgement is enacted with the real mum and the maid having to tug the child out of the circle, the maid can't bear to hurt the child so stops pulling and lets the child go to the real mother. The judge decides that this is an act of true love and therefore the maid will make the better mother and she should keep the child. All of this is set as a play within a play, where a group of villagers are arguing over who should use the land – cheese-makers or fruit-growers – people who have traditionally done it or people who believe they can feed more people.

At the beginning of the play I was convinced the cheese-makers should get the land, by the end of the play it made perfect sense that the fruit-

growers should have it. What amazed me was that a play could make me change my mind. I was totally bowled over by the fact that I was admonishing myself for being so stupid as to think the cheese-makers should get the land in the first place. I remember being astonished that a play had made me think again. If there was ever a moment when a work of art or a book or a play affected my life, that was it.

I think I have probably spent most of my performing life trying in some way or another to get people to change their minds, to look at something differently and to challenge the orthodox way of seeing. That and tell the ultimate knob gag.

Mark Thomas

just ridiculed. It also has to do with the people writing about pop music now, they're Thatcher's kids and they were bludgeoned at 10 years old with an extremely conservative 'fuck you I'm fire-proof' view. More and more people get ridiculed as pop music is editorialised by people who have a very conservative view, and a very cynical view too."

The one thing you could never accuse Jake of is cynicism. He never sneers and doesn't take the old man view that punk rock was the last big creative explosion.

"I hardly went to gigs until the acid drug culture stuff, then I started going to dance halls again. It was just like punk rock, meeting all these new people, everybody converging. What I liked about house was that people didn't pay attention to groups, they paid attention to each other. And dancing was something I'd never really done: when I was a kid before punk rock I used to go to dance halls and pose in my flares and my stuart brogues, so I found it a completely liberating experience to go and dance for ten hours.

"What's so good about house music now is that it's constantly reinventing itself... for example Marcel Halls who makes 12 different records in 12 different names, some of them world-wide smashes, could walk down the street and nobody would recognise him. Same with Tod Terry and Dave Morales – interestingly enough these guys are all getting up to 50 now and nobody cares. It's another area of pop which isn't measured in age."

I ask Jake to cite a pop group he admires beyond all others and he goes for the Velvet Underground.

"The Velvets are my Beatles. To me the Velvet Underground are the greatest rock group ever. They changed record to record and came from a very highbrow literary art background, they were all graduates and their approach to pop music was completely different from everyone else's. They're so melodic and beautiful but at the same time they're so harsh and black and brutal and dirty. Perfect example is 'Venus in Furs' and 'Here She Comes Now', beautiful melodic music with really dark undertones. The Beatles were the same, it's just a question of personal preference. I don't know anyone who can turn round and say 'The Beatles don't mean shit to me.' Look at 'Eleanor Rigby', it's so pure and sad, they're full of Larkin and TS Eliot, there's all these great voices in there."

The Velvet Underground and the Beatles are examples of the cream rising but 'quality will out' is the great rock'n' roll myth. It's not how beautiful or how relevant a work of art or a piece of music is but how it's marketed and whether its producers have finance and contacts. Alabama 3 are an example of a group whose recorded and live brilliance isn't reflected in record sales.

"It's always the problem with art and politics, there's always this interstate where they're supposed to meet but don't. The problem is with reconciling what you do in the arts with how it's sold and how it's marketed. Alabama 3 are a good example of this, with Derek Birkett (One Little Indian label boss) being an old Crass punk and coming through that whole ethos, do everything yourself, own your own means of production, press your own records etc. etc. But all he's doing is accumulating and his groups are either written off as tax losses or just grist to the mill and he's just talking in terms of surplus value too the way the bosses are. Everybody ends up being caught up in this kind of vicious circle where it's really difficult to reconcile the work with the way it's produced and the way it's marketed and the way people get to hear it." ✖

COUNTRY OF ORIGIN

by Rob Newman

an extract from a novel in progress

They were leased light industrial units on the Harmondsworth Industrial Estate. They were all acronyms that not even the person who abbreviated them understood. It was the alphabet gone mad; one syllable names that were as phonetically ugly as the buildings themselves.

D.A. and J.A., however, were different from the other buildings in the crumbling, four-acre business park. D.A. and J.A. were surrounded by high, steel fences topped by coils of razor wire. D.A. and J.A. were secured by electronic gates, uniformed guards and a kennel full of dogs. In both D.A. and J.A., you might suppose, was a workforce who could get seriously out of hand; who were not being paid nearly enough; who must have been enduring intolerable working conditions for some time. Labour standards were far worse than any of the other profit-making concerns on the Harmondworth Industrial Estate. It would, therefore, come as a surprise to discover just how many active trade unionists there were in both D.A. and J.A.

Before Sodexo's refugee mega-prison opened at Harmondsworth (that families might be all locked up together for the first time since The Poor Law), and before Sodexo's dividends started City analysts wondering whether refugees might be bigger than dot.com; there was D.A. and J.A.

D.A. was a cramped 1920s building which had once been council offices. No-one stayed in D.A longer than it took to blu-tac a crayon drawing of the last Queen of Estonia on the wall (next to Ogoni village, Albanian boyfriend and red Ferrari). From here you would be ghosted to Belmarsh or Rochester, Campsfield or Oakington and then back

again to Harmondsworth D.A., before Wackenhut took you to Heathrow. British Airways, whose tinted-glass offices overlooked the Harmondsworth Industrial Estate, had the monopoly on this lucrative human traffic; flying you out on a snake-head-return to Kinshassa, Istanbul, Tehran, Ankara or Bogota and delivering you safe into the hands of the security services in your country of origin. (From whom you had nothing to fear because we sold arms to them, so they couldn't be all bad.)

J.A. was a long, thin Nissen hut. If you went from D.A. to J.A. you might be here for a bit longer. (There was a small exercise yard in J.A). But then again you might not. You never knew. Some men and women spent less time in J.A. than D.A. Five months or five minutes. You never knew. But usually a transfer across the light industrial estate from J.A. to D.A. meant you'd be in detention for a bit longer.

Daniel watched a tall, blond, lone Ukrainian with a mighty scar on his forehead playing basketball in the sagging nets with a foam ball.

Daniel stood in front of the photocopied picture menu. Halal. Traditional British. Afro-Caribbean.

Salad. It was still two hours before dinner.

Daniel bounced a tennis ball he had found. The tennis ball had a phone number written on it.

Daniel plucked and shredded leaves of bramble and chickweed and saw himself doing it.

A Boeing stormed out of Heathrow (as executives flew off to inspect the green shoots of weak unions and job insecurity).

In J.A., crouching to look at a gap in the wooden fence (which was in front of the chain-link fence which was in front of the steel-mesh fence), Daniel watched the new jail being built a hundred yards away.

In Market Haven's police station car park Daniel had sat in the back of a Sodexo van, a Peugot Boxer. He was in a cage. There was a bolted grille of bonded mesh between him and the rear doors, and another between him and the front seats. (The lion goes from strength to strength.) There were no side-doors and the small windows were blacked-out, too. After three hours he'd been joined in the cage by a Colombian. They didn't greet each other, didn't look at each other and didn't speak. Twenty miles later, the Colombian began out of nowhere:

"Every week I go to the police station and I sign the register of aliens. Every week for six months I do this. For six months! Today I go in and they tell me my application has been turned

down, then they put me in handcuffs and throw me in this van. They don't let me go home and pack and collect my clothes, my money, my toothbrush, my soap, my address book, nothing. No, it's 'In the van! Now!'"

He'd said nothing more for the rest of the ride.

Daniel climbed on the window-sill in his tiny room and looked at a cornfield through the bars. Fish stew and dumplings, he thought.

"Daniel Chancosa!" called a guard from the office in the hall. Daniel went into the little office. The guard had a grey quiff and a black packet of Raffles in the chest pocket of his light-blue Burns Security shirt. Daniel tried to decipher the faded-blue tattoos on his forearms. The guard squinted through his cigarette smoke while he found the page he was looking for. He flattened the book out on the table-top like it was never going to be used again, then met Daniel's eyes and said: "Here."

Daniel read the Spanish phrase a sovereign-ring-finger was pointing at: Your removal order is for tomorrow.

"At eight a.m." said the guard, holding up all the fingers not holding a fag.

"That's when you're removed. Eight."

"Mexico?"

The guard flipped over a page for the phrase he was looking for. Daniel read: Country of origin. ✖

"What's the point in experience if you miss the meaning?"

Sic shares tea and buns with Sivanandan and Jenny Bourne

" am always guided by a famous thing that Camus said," explains Sivanandan halfway through our conversation. "Camus was writing to a German friend during the war, and this German friend had become a Nazi and he wrote to him and said: 'I want to destroy you in your power without mutilating you in your soul'."

Sivanandan manages to sound unpretentious whilst quoting Dylan Thomas and Pindar between sips of tea. He throws art and ideas into conversations the way other people chuck in "Y'know what I mean?" and he makes you want to read writers you've never even heard of. Sivanandan is an activist who thinks like a poet. A critic who creates; his writing slices through to the core of whatever he's dealing with, whether it's the racism directed at refugees or capitalism rewarding the few at the expense of the many. He's polite and friendly but not soft, and despite having a huge impact on Britain's radical politics he's nowhere near becoming a household name. Asian Dub Foundation sampled him for their last album *Community Music* but he's unlikely to turn up on stage and take a bow. Now in his late seventies Sivanandan hasn't courted fame.

If Sivanandan is not as well known as some left-wing figures, it is because his politics are too uncompromising for the mainstream media. His essays had an influence way beyond their initial print runs: circulated as dog-eared photocopies, they were the focus of intense political dispute. (They have since been collected and published in two volumes.) Sivanandan has always addressed the essential dilemma of how to fight without loss of humanity. Returning to Camus, Sivanandan shakes his head and says: "How will I fight a political enemy? How will I shoot my reactionary father but with a tear in my eye?" How indeed.

It would be unfair to talk about Sivanandan without bringing in Jenny Bourne and Hazel Waters. The three of them are a collective and the backbone of the Institute of Race Relations; a respectable title for a radical organisation which, in fact, used to be very establishment before it was hijacked by Bourne, Waters, Sivanandan and other workers in the early seventies. They also produce *Race and Class*, a quarterly offshoot of the IRR edited by Sivanandan, which has drawn in some of the most significant political and intellectual thinkers of the post-war period. Those who have sat on its editorial working committee or council include John Berger, Edward Said and Orlando Letelier, Allende's ambassador to the US, who was subsequently assassinated. Contributors have included Noam Chomsky, EP Thompson and Angela Davis.

Part of what's important about Sivanandan is that he understands and promotes working collectively. The IRR regularly holds seminars where activists, thinkers, artists and writers meet up; after September 11th they organised a series of discussions introduced by Sivanandan and Naomi Klein, the result of which was a collection of essays published in the summer on the Challenges of September 11th. Just as the Beatles and the Sex Pistols produced their best work when they were surrounded by radicals, musicians and artists, Sivanandan continues to be relevant because he's always willing to work with others. How many other sectagenarians appear on a subversive pop album?

Ambalavaner Sivanandan was born to a Tamil family on 20th December 1923 in Colombo, Sri Lanka (then Ceylon).

His father, whom he writes about in his novel *When Memory Dies*, was originally from a peasant family and had worked his way up to the rank of Postmaster. His sense of honour and his way of always fighting for the rights of others was a huge influence on Sivanandan but he was intolerant of mixed marriages. When Sivanandan fell in love with and married a Catholic Sinhalese girl, father and son were estranged for years. Sivanandan was politically active at university and taught briefly before going into banking. He got a job as a bank manager but it didn't quite fit him:

"I became a bank manager because I had to help my brothers and sisters, my whole family, out of poverty," says Sivanandan. "So that my politics had receded except that I helped to start a bank clerks' union even when I was a bank manager, so that rebellious tendency was still there."

The outbreak of the government-sponsored Sinhalese pogroms against Tamils in 1958 changed the course of Sivanandan's life. During the violence he had to dress as a policeman to lead his family through the mob to safety. Sickened by the hatred around him, he escaped to the UK with his wife and three kids, landing into the midst of the Notting Hill riots in London.

"That was my Damascene conversion if you like," says Sivanandan of the Notting Hill riots. "At that point the visceral, the political and the emotional and all that came together and I hated what human beings were doing to each other, and so I decided that I won't go into banking, I won't go into the jobs I'd done... I want to fight racism, I want to fight colonialism... you know the sort of young man's dream of fighting all the injustices of the world."

London didn't provide a warm welcome for the Sri Lankan refugees.

Sivanandan got a job as a tea boy in a library and his wife took work as a typist and together with their three kids they shared one room. The marriage didn't survive the strain and Sivanandan was left with the children. "I didn't even know how to cook when my wife left... bringing up children alone made a woman out of me."

'No blacks, coloureds or Irish' notices were still in the windows of London boarding houses. Then – as today – refugees weren't made welcome. "I lived in Notting Hill for a while in rented accommodation where they put all the blacks into the basement. I had terrible experiences. Then I answered an advertisement in the *New Statesman* about renting a flat in Chalk Farm, I rang up this lady and I thought '*New Statesman*; my sort of journal, on the left, fellow socialists... ' and I rang up this lady who was renting out the flat, and because by this time I knew that there was so much racism around. I started off by saying 'I am from Ceylon, and I would like to rent out this flat,' and she said, 'Er, I'm not prejudiced about you being from Ceylon or anything like that but you did say that you had three children?' And I said, 'Yes.' And she said, 'Oh well we have only two bedrooms and I don't think it's enough. So I'm sorry we can't rent it to you.' This was such a humbug answer that I rang up half an hour later, absolutely livid and I said, 'It's me again, please can I have the flat now?' And she said 'What has changed?' And I said 'I've murdered one of the little buggers!'"

This absolute refusal to accept flannel and half-truths is what marks Sivanandan out. Part of the reason he came to Britain in the first place was because he'd been educated under British colonial rule with the line that Britain somehow stood for higher values of fairness and justice:

"The British ideals were our ideals: free speech, democracy, humanitarianism, all the universal values of modernism. All the enlightenment stuff, we bought it... but I also knew that the reality was not quite right back home but when I came here it was a staggering realisation that the

SICNOTES

Both my partner's grandparents answered the Spanish Republic's call for international solidarity in 1936 and it was there that they met, fell in love and later returned to marry. They met in the hospital where her gran, Barbara, was working as a nurse and where her grandfather, John, recovered after being shot. Now that was what I call a life-changing moment!

The story brought to life the heroism and commitment of that generation and made real the struggle against Franco. It seemed to provide a tangible measuring stick by which I could compare my own more humble contributions. The unfortunate consequence of this was that it fostered a rather unhealthy fantasy with the epic or grand gesture that I think is common to many revolutionaries.

It was not until I met John's sister that this rather distorted view of commitment was finally shattered. We had been talking about politics, communism, anarchism, the Spanish Civil War when I casually remarked about how heroic and committed I thought her brother had been to travel across Europe to fight with the International Brigades. Deep down I think I was trying to impress her, steal a bit of reflected glory, that had it been me in that situation I would have done the same... sure, words are cheap!

"No!" she replied fiercely, "what was heroic about John was that all his life, from the day he was born to the day he died, he filled every moment with some kind of useful activity. Going to Spain was just one example, but what was really important was that he never wasted time, he was always reading, educating himself, involving himself in projects. That was heroic."

And I looked at myself, humbled and realised I'd been waiting around for my fantasised moment with destiny for too long.

Matt Hannan

"We were having to learn how to deal with and politicise each other. Every day something would change, somebody would come with a bribe, offer to publish someone's first novel, buy the library off... so everything that happened was politics"

reality was completely different, in fact the opposite. I suppose in a way it is a very ironical thing; our fight ever since has been to return to Britain the values which it preached to us without itself practising them. That may sound a little pretentious. That is where British imperialism, British colonialism made a mistake; the values that they taught us and didn't live up to became our values and we took it so seriously that we now challenged Britain to live up to them."

Sivanandan qualified as a librarian in 1964, and was employed two years later by the Institute of Race Relations, an organisation dedicated to the study of race relations. Originally a branch of the Royal Institute of International Affairs, the IRR was funded by big business – Shell, Nuffield, Rockefeller and Ford among others. The IRR was supposed to be devoted to the objective study of race relations. After the 1962 Immigration Act it began to take the government's view that controlling immigration was necessary to improve race relations. Most of the early studies looked into Africa and other newly developing countries with a view to seeing how business could invest there.

Sivanandan took a pay cut to take the job at the Institute because he understood that it was open to subversion.

"There was an air of genteel decay about the whole Institute when I went for the interview. People on the council were the lords and ladies of humankind, these were the people who had ruled me and my country. So I already had an understanding of what they were up to. I felt that I must – to use Pindar's beautiful phrase – 'exhaust the limits of the possible.' I cannot shake the world but I can move pebbles which might bring on an avalanche."

"We had people saying things like 'we need to have fewer of them for better race relations'," adds Jenny Bourne who went to the Institute as a researcher in the late '60s. "They were also saying 'Unless we make the situation right we're going to have social dislocation, which will cause problems and that will be bad for the nation. Not bad for the victims but bad for the nation'."

In 1972, Sivanandan and his allies led a coup against the old guard. Their plan was to create a new IRR: "a sort of think-tank, a think-in-order-to-do-tank for black and third world peoples".

"It was a Pyhrric victory," says Sivanandan. "We won the battle for the Institute but the management council had the money and they left with it. They left us with the lifeboat. So we moved to an old warehouse here in Kings Cross, and a lot of the black community supported us during the struggle, putting out leaflets about it and so on and so forth, so we got them to move the library and they kept the library open in the evenings for themselves, so the library became a very important part of education of black people."

The run-up to the bloodless coup was a political struggle which saw the state and the Institute's council try to stave off the mutiny with bribes and threats. "So we were having to learn how to deal with and politicise each other," says Jenny Bourne. "And every day something would change, somebody would come with a bribe, offer to publish someone's first novel, buy the library off... so everything that happened was politics. It was a very happening place."

In the midst of fighting for control of the Institute the workers were also closely involved with the Black Panthers and welfare programs. "We were trusted by the black community and then the black community was on form," says Sivanandan. "We were actually given money by a big London charity to kind of, on their behalf, give it out to black groups," says Jenny Bourne. "They didn't know how to relate to black people so they needed us as pimps. In that way we managed to fund quite a lot of welfare work being done by the black power movement."

"We managed to change the whole way the Institute had been run internally," she adds. "When I'd gone there it was completely hierarchical. I was on the bottom, the only people below me were the people who answered the door and answered the telephone. Everybody was kept in their place, we were not allowed to go to council meetings, it was too frightening for us to talk at staff meetings... to me the most important thing was that we began to be able to run the Institute collectively, and it was a real collective where we all knew each other's strengths and weaknesses and all helped each other to grow, to change and to grow along with the Institute, so we could all do what we wanted in the best

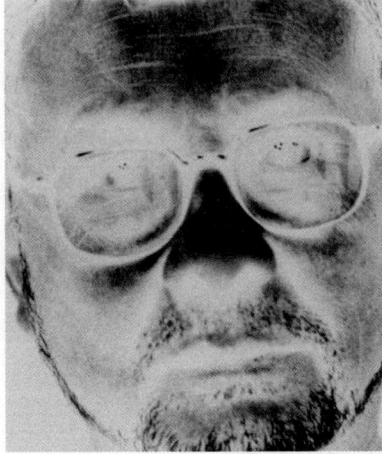

way for the organisation and for ourselves. And that, to me, was an important political development. A lot of people talked about being a collective in a kind of mouthy sort of way, but I think we really were."

After hijacking the Institute they set up *Race and Class* and appointed Sivanandan as editor. Various academics who'd been supportive during the storming of the Institute's gates were incensed that a librarian (and a former tea boy at that) was going to edit a radical journal. That was a post they had their own eyes on. So the next fight was against those who wanted control of *Race and Class* for their own ends. They threw all the academics off the board and invited the radicals in.

"What happened was really important for my politics," says Jenny Bourne. "This journal which was called *Race* and really boring, we turned it into *Race and Class*. It was a third world journal which looked to all these liberation movements. We brought in a whole lot of people that we'd met; people who'd been involved in liberation movements, some of the greatest people on the left throughout the world. I actually think I have been honoured to have been working with those people after 1974, and getting them involved in our struggle and that in a way gave us a whole new perspective."

Sivanandan proved to be a great editor and essayist. Like many great essayists, Sivanandan's best work is always a form of attack. Many credit him with the demise of racism awareness training – fashionable in many liberal and left-leaning authorities in the early 1980s – which he demolished in his essay 'RAT and the Degradation of Black Struggle'. Whilst others were saying that the root of all problems was language and the way it was used, Sivanandan pointed out that as long as black people were economically disadvantaged, trapped in ghettos and scapegoated under capitalism, then concentrating on labels was something of a side issue. And one that provided jobs for black professionals but was politically damaging to the community as a whole. His 1990 essay, 'All that Melts into Air is Solid', a stinging attack on the trendy betrayals and selfish limitations of the new left gathered around the once-popular magazine *Marxism Today*, remains one of the most substantial and influential attempts on the left to halt the drift towards consumerism and compromise. While *Marxism Today* pronounced the fall of the Soviet Bloc as 'the end of history' and claimed that we should all embrace capitalism, Sivanandan argued that history was an ongoing battle and that those living in degradation and poverty didn't view capitalism as an all-conquering hero. After *Marxism Today* had shut up shop, ex-editor Martin Jacques appeared on TV claiming that the 'tiger economies' and Asian-style capitalism was the way forward. A

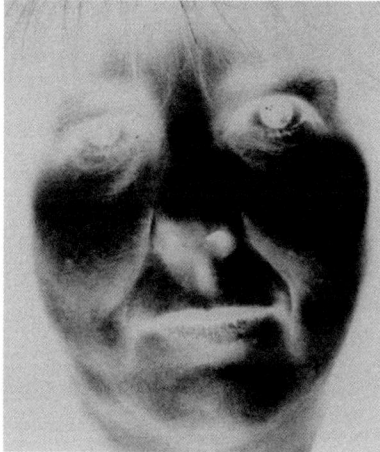

month later the 'way forward' collapsed when the tiger economies crumbled and Sivanandan was vindicated once again.

One criticism made of Sivanandan by the left establishment is that he's out of time and that New Labour rather than struggle is the way forward. The problem isn't that he's anachronistic but that he's ahead of his time. He was one of the earliest critics of globalisation, bringing it to the fore as early as 1979.

"I wrote a pamphlet on imperialism in the silicon age which was a paper that I gave at a conference in Berlin. That was the first time I got up and talked about the new certainties of globalisation, about how capital was moving."

Activist and scholar Edward Said has pointed out that immigration is the symbol of the 20th century, saying that if you want to look at what capitalism does to people's lives, look to migration. In the last half of the 20th century there have been vast numbers of people dislocated by war, famine and economics. As politicians throughout Europe continue to scapegoat refugees, Sivanandan has rightly argued that the distinction between economic and political refugees is bogus.

"Globalisation displaces people, I call it economic genocide by stealth. There's no such thing as an illegal migrant, there's only an illegal government. And those illegal governments are our governments back home which have been set up by Western capital. So if you have a politics, a global pro-multinational politics of the West, which sets up puppet dictatorships, reactionary regimes – or if it doesn't set them up it maintains, or helps finance these regimes in the interests of oil, in the interests of getting cheap labour, in the interests of multinational corporations – then if you go over to the third world and set up these regimes and they become politically repressive, then obviously the people who are being oppressed have got to get out of that country. So it is your economics, the governments of multinational corporations, that makes for our politics, which makes the migrant come over here. So he's not an economic migrant, he's a political migrant. You can't distinguish in our third world countries between the politics and economics; the politics is the economics.

"The west is quite happy to take in economic migrants if they are businessmen (with the requisite £250,000), professionals, or technologically-skilled. It welcomes the computer wizards of Silicon Valley of Bangalore but does not want the persecuted peoples of Sri Lanka or the Punjab."

Hostility towards refugees is no longer colour-coded; people don't have to be black to be poor, they just have to be born at the wrong time, in the wrong place under an unjust system. The

> "The west is quite happy to take in economic migrants if they are businessmen, professionals, or technologically-skilled. It welcomes the computer wizards of Silicon Valley of Bangalore but does not want the persecuted peoples of Sri Lanka or the Punjab"

Balkanisation of countries, where nations split into hostile factions, has resulted in floods of refugees. They are often discriminated against on the grounds of poverty and the term that's bandied around to describe the hatred directed at them is 'xenophobia: the fear of strangers.'

"I've always rejected the term xenophobia because it's a harmless sort of word for a very harmful attitude. What is xenophobia? Fear of strangers. Third world people never had fear of strangers; it's European white people who had fear of strangers. There's a famous saying about Africa: 'The missionaries came to Africa with a bible in one hand, but when they left they left the bible and took the land.' So there's no fear for us of being hospitable to strangers; it's a European disease. Also xenophobia has the innocuous look of something that is natural; it's as if it's natural to be afraid of strangers who are unusual and not used to your manners or your circumstances...

"In the act of using the word xenophobia, it detracts from the seriousness of the whole thing, so what we have said is, that it is xeno – fear of strangers in form, but racist in content. You don't have to have a black face to be poor, from the Balkans if you like, not wanted... so what we're having now in the global arena is xenoracism.

"It's demonisation. The cultural demonisation of asylum seekers takes place before the law comes into place. Capitalism moves in mysterious ways, its miracles to perform. There's a collective subconscious about capitalism which allows it to use the cultural feeling, the cultural instance, the cultural dynamics of a people in order to soften them up for the economic exploitation to come. In an old democracy like Britain it's a blotting paper society that absorbs and negates opposition."

Culturally the Arab world is seen as 'the other' and so the plight of the Palestinians under Israeli apartheid has long been ignored and glossed over.

"If you have experience of being oppressed as a movement that must open you up to the oppression of me as a black man, otherwise what is the point of having the experience and missing the meaning? The situation in Zionist Israel is exactly that. These are people who have suffered so long and so terribly and yet these are the people themselves who are becoming the oppressors. What's the point in experience if you miss the meaning? And that's where Camus' thought comes in, that it is why we must destroy people in their power but not mutilate their soul."

According to Sivanandan, America's reaction to September 11th is a classic example of not learning lessons. "The world is in danger from America – economically, politically and, now, militarily. Globalisation has engendered a monolithic economic system governed by American corporations that hold nations in thrall. September 11th has engendered a monolithic political culture that holds that those who are not pro-American are either terrorists or value-less and therefore surplus to civilisation. Together, they signal the end of civil society and the beginnings of a new imperialism, brutal and unashamed.

"On a more philosophical level, one would have expected that the suffering inflicted on the American people after September 11th would have sensitised them to the suffering of the poor and the deprived of the world. But, alas, they have had the experience and missed the meaning. Worse, they have denied all meaning to their own suffering by inflicting it upon others.

"We are connected to one another, in the deepest sense, through our common pain. When we lose that connection we lose our humanity."

All the way through our conversation Sivanandan kept stopping to ask if I needed more tea, to ask his colleagues if they'd ordered their sandwiches, to make sure they weren't waiting for him to finish the interview before they had their lunch. I had a cold and it was all I could do to stop him from making me a hot Lemsip. He never acts like a big shot; treating people well is part of his nature as well as his politics. Sivanandan believes he's kept his humanity by battling for the rights of others. The IRR is as well known for highlighting the deaths in police custody and abuses of power as it is for pushing radical thought forward through *Race and Class*. You could never accuse Sivanandan and his colleagues of ignoring the big picture or missing the all-important human details. The thing about Sivanandan is that whether he's quoting literature or exposing the Emperor's new clothes, he always makes sense and he always takes politics back to the effect on people's lives. That's what's important to him; what the decisions made up on high actually mean in Brixton or in the sweat-shops of Indonesia. He's blunt, sharp and ferocious and loves art and friends as much as he hates what people are capable of doing to each other. He's expansive and warm but he's also an attack terrier. Over the years he's developed a reputation for being clear-headed and incorruptible. He's the antithesis of those obsessed with fame and financial gain and if he does appear in the media it is always to make a point rather than to sell himself.

"I learned to reply in a way that they wouldn't edit me out like the David Dimbleby programmes after the '81 riots, and on some other programme about the Scarman Report. Because there is a way of talking where everything you say is so loaded, everything you say counts. So that was a very good discipline for me.

"I think I always felt that I should be known by my work and not by who I am. Secondly, I always thought that as a director of the institute and the editor of *Race and Class*, the most important thing about power is not to use it.

"I suppose I'm arrogant but not vain and there is a distinction. I think vain people become celebrities; arrogant people don't need it. It's like God he makes the rain and the world in six days and rests on Sunday. I know who I am. I don't need somebody else to tell me who I am. I think celebrities need that; they need acceptance, they need to be validated." ✖

SICNOTES

FREAKS

'Gooble gobble, gooble gobble, we accept ya, we accept ya, one of us...' The words sung by a group of circus freaks at a wedding between one of them, and a 'normal' woman, in the seminal film from 1932, *Freaks*. Using real freak show performers of the time, it still stands as the Hollywood film with the most disabled performers in it. Ever. Now there are virtually no disabled people on our screens at all. If we see one, it's invariably played by a non-disabled actor (swiftly followed by an award: Ugh.). The end image of the Freaks crawling in the mud, to kill the man oppressing them, is one of my all-time favourites in cinema. A metaphor for society's treatment of us, for Hollyweird's attitude to us, and the shock of seeing so many real disabled people on screen is more powerful now than it was then. WHY? Because we have been systematically removed from mainscreen life, sanitised to help the stupid, and our real lives replaced by bad actors and worse scripts. Well, fuck *Rainman*, *Forrest Gump*, Gina McKee in *Notting Hill* etc... I want the real thing, in our glorious, different, talented beauty... They crawled in the mud, and we'll never give up.

Matt Fraser

Kalvin Clein

for freezing goolies

Bobby Owens

by Johnny Brown

I had this mate called John Fairs who used to put on the early Resurrection do's when it was at the Mayfair in Newcastle. A top lad John; good looking kid, always making the right moves. A brilliant surfer and snowboarder, he's gone on to other things now. He tour manages the Prodigy and shacks up with the aristocracy and lives next door to Tony Blair. But back when the Res was kicking he was just starting to put the contacts together and obviously looking to impress folk. So he throws a party and invites loads of his new industry bod mates up from London. Ten thirty pm Saturday night and the wine's in the fridge, the crates of beer are on the table and DJ Conas is setting up in the front room.

John's got this great flat in Tynemouth overlooking the sea. King Eddie's Bay where him and his mates have surfed since they were kids; you can see the outline of the old priory lit up on this dark winter's night, nothing better to impress the bods from down south. The UV backdrops go up and a bit of a video projection, fractal dolphins snowboarding through aqua blue tunnels – that sort of thing. Someone sticks some silver foil over the windows which looks very Andy Warhol and all the toe-rags from North Shields and Cullercoats have been banned, just in case like.

"D'you think that's a good idea John?" someone says. "I mean, you know most of them, a lot of them are your mates."

"Yeah, but what kind of mates are they, know what I mean? They turn up whacked out of their heads with no booze, drink whatever's there, put a heavy macho vibe on the place, puke all over, and then start fighting, and that's just the lasses."

"Aye but still John, you've known most of them for a long time, you know

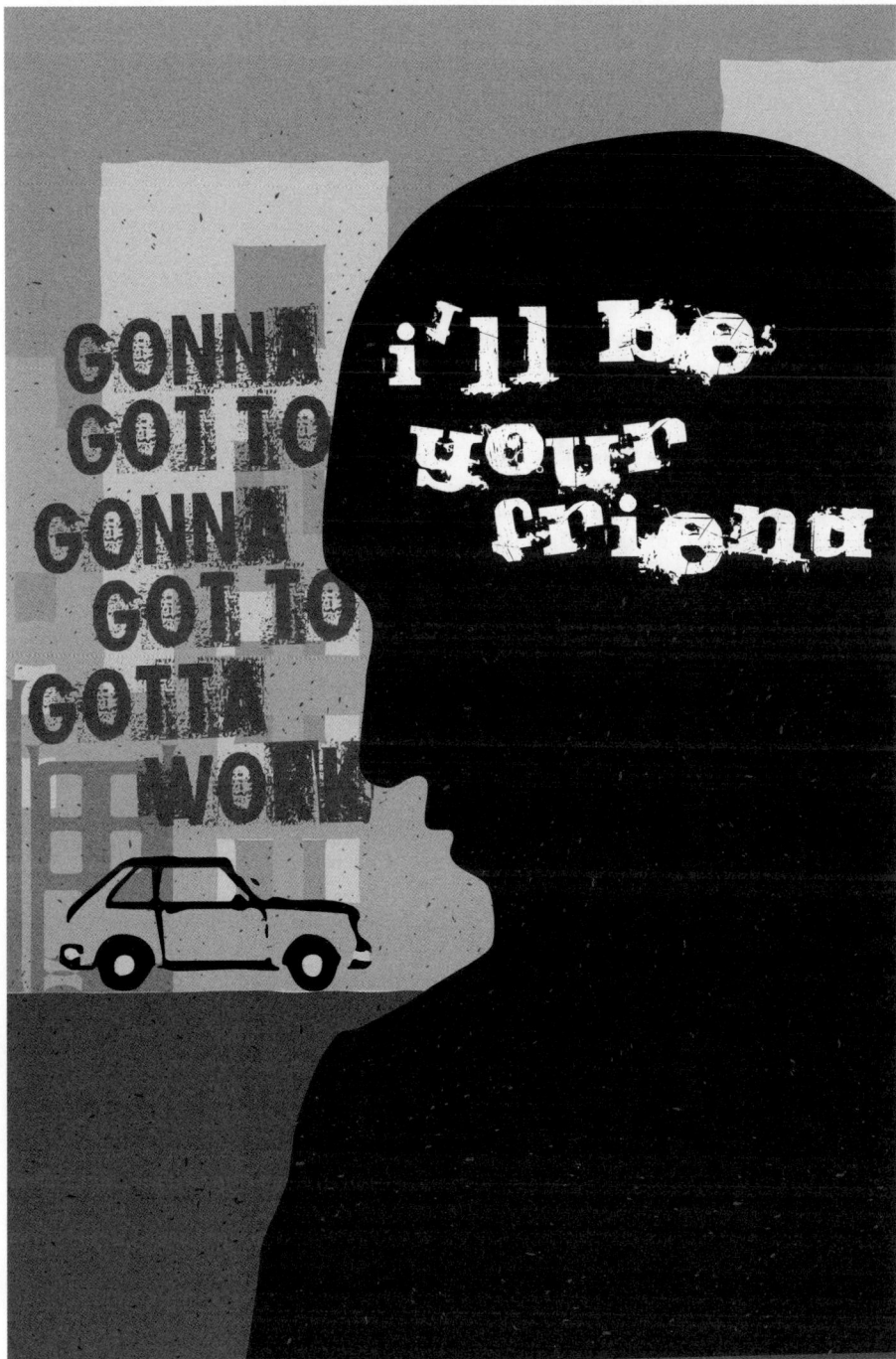

what it's like round here, they'll be well offended if they think they've been knocked back."

"Aye but not half as offensive as I know they'll be to me mates from London. Fuck that, I'm not having those animals spoil my reputation."

"Well if you look at it that way."

"I am, hey man, it only takes one knacker and that's it. I've got a lot of influential people coming up and I want them to experience Geordie hospitality, not Geordie hospitals."

Someone asks us what we think, but we don't have an opinion. John's party, John's prerogative; simple as that. Anyway, there are plenty of goodies floating about and the stage looks set for a champion little party. There's only one thing missing: ROBERT OWENS!

"Does anyone fancy nipping down to Middlesbrough to pick up Robert Owens?"

He looks towards his usual runner, DJ Conas. DJ Conas sniffs.

"Well if it was Carl Cox I might consider it, but Robert Owens... "

He looks away in disdain. Hardcore, Conas knows the fuckin' score.

John appeals to his better side.

"Ah howay, Conas."

He's stubborn as fuck, Conas though, if he doesn't want to do a thing that's it; game over. Besides he's got a set to work out.

"Besides I've got a set to work out."

Too right. It's a big night for the lad. London bods coming up and what have you. He wants to play, wants to put on a show, can't be doing with running round after other DJs. Conas retreats to a corner and sits on his record box. He busies himself with building a spliff and keeps his head right down. So that's the end of that.

"Fuckin' hell! ROBERT OWENS is playing down the road at the Arena in Middlesbrough. AND NO-ONE IS WILLING TO GO AND PICK HIM UP."

I look at me best mate Chess and Chess looks at me.

ROBERT OWENS = I'LL BE YOUR FRIEND = GOD!

We'll go.

"I'll get yous on the guest list and all that," says John

"Fine, we're there John, we're there."

"Look after him mind."

"Whee aye John, course we will."

"Dont abuse him or nowt."

"Nah nah, don't be silly, we'll look after him."

"I promised him Pure Geordie Hospitality and all that, make sure you give it to him."

"John, don't worry we'll look after him."

John gets straight on to the blower. Five minutes later we're guestlisted up and within six we're in Chess's Volvo Estate and tooling down the A18, or whatever road to Middlesbrough it is. It's a beautiful cold night, clear sky, stars and what have you. Teesside is thirty miles away, we neck a dove each as we go under the Tyne Tunnel. It only takes 20 minutes or something to get to Middlesbrough and the place looks simply awesome as we hit the flyover that cuts over the ICI plant; all shiny refineries stretching away into infinity, purple clouds of smoke billowing up into the ether. Chemical world and no mistake.

We park up on a bit of wasteland behind the club and Chess builds a couple of spliffs. Just for Bobby like; he's bound to want to chill when he gets off the decks. We'll give him these as soon as we get back in the car. Chess has skunk joints for breakfast, the cottage industry stuff that's grown in council houses throughout the country. I watch him as he packs these two. I've got that little buzz in the back of my head.

Expectation, as ever, is all.

That should sort him out.

We enter the Arena.

It's rammed downstairs. This is post 'Hit Man and Her' time when the High Street was really starting to show its face on the scene but Boro's always had clued-up clubs surrounding it like the Tall Trees and the Country Club on a Sunday where you'd get punters from all over the north congregating. It's also always had top clothes shops so consequently all the designers that defined that certain time are on show; Moschino and Richmond, shiny shirts and all that palaver. The clubs made a bit of an effort too; the usual shite film set scenario designed to lull the punters into a false sense of luxury and prise more money out of them. I'm arsed if I can remember which particular theme but we're probably talking Mock Roman Empire exotica, pillars round the club with plaster elephants hanging off them, you know what I mean; bowls of fruit tumbling out of girls' cleavages. Nero fiddling in the cash box whilst the money tills burn, Caligula snorting snide cocaine in the ladies toilets and Jeremy Healy is on the decks in the main room, probably.

Bob – we are told – is playing in the smaller upstairs room. We bound up the stairs. And there he is:

ROBERT OWENS = I'LL BE YOUR FRIEND = GOD.

He's on the decks spinning away, beatific smile on his face. We get straight down the front and groove away, well Chess grooves away, I just shuffle, out of time, like I always do, like I always will. But I'm bang into it, bang into the night, bang into Middlesbrough, bang into all these boys and girls around me. Bang into me best mate, Chess, bang into the things we've done in the past, bang into the things we'll do in the future. Bang into Bobby as he gives out all the love up there. He's got a record out at this time, a brilliant garagey thing called GOTTA WORK. All of a sudden he's mixed it in and he's pulled this fuckin' microphone out and he's singing along to it.

SINGING ALONG TO HIS OWN RECORD. (I tell you, you can stick all that Carl Cox three deck stuff right up your arse. Singing along to your own record and making little pretend scratchy motions as you mix the records in and out. Thats where it's at, kidda). Outlandish cheesy bit of showbiz cheek really, but he pulls it off. He just sticks on a word or a sentence like he does in 'I'll Be Your Friend'.

I'M GONNA WORK
I GOTTA WORK
I'M GONNA WORK
I GOTTA WORK
GONNA
GOT TO
GONNA.
GOT TO
GOTTA WORK

Total repetition, Soul mantra. A church organ is gliding over the beat. It's holy this shit. He closes his eyes and takes us into the heavens, well, I can't speak for anyone else like, but he takes me right up there. Great Dove too, let's have another one, why not? It's one of those nights and its going to get better.

But before you know it the night has ended and the lights are up and the bouncers are closing in and you're tripping over the empty Pils bottles on the floor. And you can see the paint peeling off the plaster elephants, the pillars are plastic and the fruit in the bowls of the women's cleavage has turned rank all of a sudden. Yep, the money's on the other side of the bar now. It's that licensing law time of night. Bedtime for straights.

Not for us though, we're off to a party, with Robert Owens, fuckin right.

We approach the decks and introduce ourselves.

"Hi Robert, we're Chess and Johny, friends of John Fairs, we've come to give you a lift up to the party."

"Oh guys, HI, We thought you guys weren't going to make it, didn't we Jackie? Hey guys, meet Jackie – she's my manager."

Jackie is this totally drop dead gorgeous Nigerian woman. We say hi.

"Alright Jackie. I'm Johny, this is Chess. We've just come to pick you up, take you off to the party."

"Hey guys hi, hey why didn't you come up and introduce yourselves and have a beer, up on the podium, when Robert was doin' his shit?"

"Well, we were just down the front, getting into it like."

"Aye, fuck all that ligging shite."

"So you like the stuff that Robert's doing then?"

Pure manager is Jackie. You can see her and John getting on well.

"Aye, we love it. There's no-one quite like him."

Her eyes light up. That's what she wants to hear.

"Cool, but you still should have come and hung with us, we were like, where are these guys?"

"Yeah," chips in Bob. "We thought you guys weren't going to show or something."

Bobbie's wearing this little marine number, camp as fuck, real Chicago queen's voice. The guy is a star. There is no other word for it.

"We wouldn't miss this for the world."

We offer to carry his record boxes for him.

"Oh no guys really, I can't let you do that."

"Nah Robert, we insist."

"Well how kind. Hey Jackie, aren't these two boys like the nicest people in the world?"

"Yeah. You two are simply the nicest boys I've met since I got here."

"We're not THAT nice, Robert. Nice to be appreciated all the same."

"Aye, you're not too bad yourself like Robert."

We step over the casualties on the stairs, dodge the bouncers and carry Robert's record boxes to the boot of the

SICNOTES

My sister was born when I was nearly two. She was yellow with jaundice and covered in bruises from a long labour. I think she'd been having doubts about whether to be born at all. As soon as she could string a sentence together she began asking repeatedly "Who am I?" and "Why am I here?" No-one knew the answer, so we all just laughed, which didn't impress her. As the years went by she crusaded tirelessly at the kitchen table against the evils and injustices of the world, making such sacrifices that I wouldn't have dreamt of, like sending her pocket money to the South African Anti-Apartheid campaign. She made a shrine to Steve Biko in our bedroom. Disarmed and belittled by her raw and powerful righteousness, I continued to snicker. When adolescence, bereavement, family dysfunction, and the cheap acid we were taking all kicked in at once, my sister could carry the weight of the world no longer and it stopped being funny. So began a battle with the mental health system that would continue throughout her teens. The official 'solution' to my sister's impossible and self-destructive behaviour was always to drug her up and lock her up. At 14, she was transformed into a zombie by her 'medication', at turns aggressive and mute. A person regarded as 'crazy' in this country automatically loses a number of basic human rights, including the right to choose and refuse treatment. That 'treatment' still includes Electro Convulsive Therapy, or electric shock treatment as it is better known, despite numerous reports of serious side-effects. Thankfully, as my sister was so young, parental car. Robert and Jackie get in the back. Chess fires up a spliff and hands it back. Robert looks a bit unsure.

"Well you know guys I don't normally smoke that shit."

"Go on Robert, it'll chill you right out."

"Aye, you deserve it after all that singing and DJing."

"Ooh, go on then. God you two are so kind."

"D'you fancy an E?"

"Woah, I think that's pushing it a bit."

"Aye alright, fair enough. You'll love this party we're taking you to anyway. John's got some Pure Geordie Hospitality laid on for you; you'll both love it. I'll just whip out on to the motorway and we'll be there in twenty minutes or so."

"Hey right, so what do you two guys do?"

"Well, I'm in antiques. Architectural antiques, know what I mean Robert? And Johny here is the best poet in Britain at the moment."

Ah no, we're off again, here's where Chess totally embarrasses me.

"Is that right, Johny?"

"Well, err, sort of."

Change the fucking subject, quick.

"So where are you based Jackie?"

"Oh, Butterfly Studios in Stockwell, London. I don't suppose you've heard of it."

"Whee aye," says Chess "Me brother Chester is Youth's best mate. We know Butterfly well."

"Yep, and I was invited to a midsummer solstice party in the KLF's back garden, once. Youth was there with his dad, standing over a pond, in which fluoro newts swam, as dry ice spread over the lawn and the Orb's pointy white balloons floated through the trees. The KLF's conceptual lamb hid itself away in a closet, flashing lights of both wisdom and fear in its eyes. Adamski walked past with a baby in his arms and hippy girls of hypemodel proportions comported themselves everywhere. It was just a moment in time, but a perfect one at that."

"We're all connections, me and Chess."

"Wow, small world guys."

"Aye. All things connect like, Jackie."

"They certainly do, so where are you guys from again?"

"North Shields."

permission was required and my mum held out. Our family was branded as unco-operative and my sister was placed in foster care for the short periods when she wasn't sectioned. She was also prescribed Lithium with the threat of detainment if she refused to take it.

When she was 18 my sister got pregnant while living in a mixed Community Care home. (The idea of sticking all the disturbed people together in one house with nothing to do has always bothered me.) Initially my mum and me were thrown into a panic but having

her daughter was the impetus my sister needed to get the 'professionals' off her back once and for all. Social workers swarmed around them like vultures waiting for a disaster to happen but it never came.

Of course, ever unpredictable, my sister has pulled it off. She straddles madness and genius on a daily basis; managing to bring up her little girl alone, on an estate in Brixton, whilst doing a degree in astro-physics at the same time. She still alarms me with her impossible questions and moral mountaineering, but while her head is in the sky

being a single mum has kept her feet firmly on the ground. It terrifies me to think of the power the mental health system had over my family and still has over the 10% of the population that are diagnosed with mental health problems. It is extremely difficult, particularly for less educated people, to stand up to doctors and those in authority and shake off the labels they like to attach. My sister is an unusual, and to me, inspiring survival story and evidence that it can be done.

Daisy Asquith

"Gee," says Robert, looking slightly worried for a moment "Ain't that where they have all the riots and stuff?"

"Well it's Tynemouth were going to, actually."

"And John's operating a very selective door policy so there'll be no riff raff like, no scumbags from Shields or Cullercoats there."

"Cool, so it'll be just like, how d'you guys say it, Pure Geordie Hospitality, right?"

"Right."

"And I just love those accents you've got, they're so, so... "

"Northern?"

"Yeah, something like that."

Chess hands the spliff back to Robert, Robert looks at it uncertainly; he's looking a bit tired as it goes, let's get him and Jackie straight to the party.

We roar out of the carpark and immediately get lost in Middlesbrough's one way system. It's a desolate scene is Boro at two in the morning with the clubs chucking out. It's the usual nightmare; blood on the pavement and sick on the shoes of knickerless girls in doorways who clutch on to battered kebabs, gagging for something you might call a shag. We just hope Robert and Jackie have got their eyes closed.

"Don't worry, as soon as we're out of Middlesbrough we'll be home in thirty minutes at the most."

The car noses into an industrial area. Prostitutes hang on the corners – why we just can't fathom though we can take a guess at the kind of bleak situation that would drive the girls out here. But what kind of desperate fucker would be out and about in weather like this? Still there they are: big girls looking like Chubby Brown in drag, implausibly short skirts on this cruel winter night. Pretty Woman it's not. Snatches of mist roll lazily across the street. We can see the flyover; it's up there, but we just can't get to the road that slips on to it. We circle below. Things are starting to twist a little, the amber lights normally so smack pretty are starting to melt and ooze into our brains. We look at each other, me and Chess, we're both thinking the same thing. Hollywood itself could not serve up a more convincing nightmare of a scene. And then, thank God, we roar up on to the motorway, right let's get the fuck out and return like homecoming heroes to the party, with Bobby Owens as our booty. Party, girls, substances, music, booze: it'll all be ours in twenty five minutes.

Like shite! A vicious, blanket fog has descended over the land. Chess cannot see an inch in front of the bonnet. I know what he's thinking.

What if I crash and we kill Robert Owens? And Jackie; far too beautiful to be killed in a car crash on Teesside, next to the refineries, which don't look so beautiful now.

CHEMICAL WORLD AND IT'S MY MISTAKE.

The two in the back are looking a little stressed out.

"Here Johny," Chess whispers viciously "Stick a fucking tape on for Christsake."

I rummage for a tape and stick it in. Ah no!

The first tune to come blaring out is – you've guessed it.

I'LL BE YOUR

I'LL BE YOUR

I'LL BE YOUR

FRIEND.

It's one of my tapes too, one of me special mixes, all crunching beats and crashing crossfades. I mean we are talking the pits of mixing, the absolute fucking pits. Chess throws me a dirty look. An auto-homicidal lorry driver whooshes past at ninety miles an hour. I picture the Volvo ad in my mind, all the sales psychology the wankers in ad-land lay on you. About the Volvo being the safest car on the road and all that. It doesn't help. I trust Chess implicitly though.

Our car shudders, Chess grits his teeth and the E decides to give the brain another little twist. Robert, thank God, seems to have fallen asleep.

I'LL BE YOUR FRIEND, FOR ALL TIME.

"Aye," says Chess to Jackie, as casual as only a dealer in architectural fireplaces can be.

"We'll be there in about, umm, forty minutes."

"Right."

"Right, and it's gonna be a great party. Definitely Jackie, a great party. Great kid John, always looks after his artists at the Res. And as I said, we'll be there in forty, forty five minutes."

"You'll love it."

"Yeah, you'll love it."

"Honestly?"

"Aye, honestly."

"Okay," says Jackie "I'm sure we will."

Two and a half hours later we emerge at the right side of the Tyne Tunnel and the mist has magically lifted. We zoom on down to the party. It's going to be worth it, definitely. We pull up outside John's, the priory all lit up behind us, waves crashing in the bay down below, we wake Robert Owens, mission accomplished.

"Okay Robert, Jackie, welcome to Tynemouth, we know you're gonna have a top time."

Not much sound from outside but we know it'll be kicking inside. We push the door open. And the sight I'm met with is definitely one of the most desolate bummed-out visions in a whole lifetime of twisted partying. One guy, slumped, comatose, in the corridor. We shrug our shoulders and smile bravely at the Jackie and Bob roadshow. Somehow we cannot look them in the eyes. We venture on down the hall gingerly stepping over the booze-ridden corpse. We check the various rooms out. Most people have clambered onto beds and cling to them like shipwrecked survivors. The London bods are in the front room.

They've brought their own tunes and have commandeered the decks. A party unto themselves. They dance on oblivious to everyone else.

Conas is sat on his record box, skinning up, looking morose, obviously

SICNOTES

More than any book or song, more even than *Naked Lunch* or 'Be Bop A Lula', the sequence of events that had the most radical effect on my thinking was the assassination of John Kennedy and the subsequent murder of alleged lone gunman Lee Oswald. Maybe I was naive, I was only sixteen at the time, but the election of JFK as President of the United States seemed like a new day dawning and the start of both a decade and an era when a young generation would start moving to power and would have its voice heard. It was the very last time that I believed that anything of any importance could be achieved within the system, or that the system itself was anything more than thin velvet over a ruthless iron fist. As a teenager I trusted Jack Kennedy. He was the bootlegger's son, but he and Nikita Khrushchev had proved themselves able to rein in the generals and halt the train of mobilisation that could have ended our world in thermo-nuclear fire. JFK created the momentum to put a man on the Moon by the end of the decade. At the time, we didn't know he was fucking Marilyn Monroe, but that alone would have made him the hero of me and my nasty little Hank B. Marvin mates. When word came from Dallas that he'd been shot, it was a tragedy. When Jack Ruby whacked out Oswald we knew it was a coup. Before all the deaths of witnesses and all the annals of conspiracy, we kids knew. The bastards had killed our man. We now fought on alone.

Mick Farren

not getting a chance to play. Obviously not wanting to say anything.

"Go on man Conas, have a crack, they're your decks."

"Nah, I don't want to put John's nose out of joint, know what I mean?"

"But you want to play, yeah?"

"Oh aye, I want to play alright."

"And you're twenty times better than the guy in the dance label flight jacket who's on the decks right now."

"Well, maybe later."

Oh dear, Party Politics, there's nowt worse. He's just too reticent for his own good, Conas. I turn to Jackie.

"It's a bit urmm, urmm"

"Intimate?" volunteers Jackie.

"And cold," says Robert.

"Ah aye, it's grim up north Robert."

Small groups huddle together in each room. John Fairs has locked himself away in his room, either in a huff or out of shame. Whatever the reason, he's in there and he won't come out. A mate called Steve Hudson comes over. He's great Hudson. Won an MBE for saving a local gangster who was drowning, surfed out and dragged him back in.

I ask him what the coup is.

"Aye, John went and banned half his mates so the other half boycotted the party. Bit of a silly move really, it's your mates who make you, isn't it?"

Well depends what you want to make, but I get your point Steve. I know it's certainly true that what makes you tends to eventually break you, but most people generally find that out for themselves.

"Bit of a miserable turn out, eh?"

"Well I've been to worse but I've never taken Robert Owens to any of them. Never mind. Hudson, Storesy, Biscuit, Conas, Deb, Shan. The company's top notch and that'll do me."

"Aye, just come into this other room Johnny and I'll sort you out with something."

Like I said: top lad Steve.

Robert fell asleep and smitten as we were, me and Chess probably (well no, we most definitely did) bored the pants off Jackie for about two hours. At about seven in the morning she suddenly remembers they have a flight back to London from Teesside Airport.

"Hey look you guys, I've got to get Robert back to Teesside Airport. D'you fancy driving me back?"

Chess suddenly looks very pale.

"I don't think I'm in a fit state to tell the truth Jackie."

Really they should just stay and chill out.

"Really you should just stay and chill out. We can go for a walk along the beach and grab some breakfast. And DJ Conas is playing Surfers, the local club. You'll love Surfers. And besides, I'm sure John'll want to see you when he comes out of his room, and Robert looks dead comfortable where he is. It'd be a shame to wake him, we can even get him some blankets."

There were a thousand good reasons why Jackie should stay but then a thousand baaad excuses came up as to why they should leave. Improbable business meetings and all that. I mean, if I was in her shoes I'd probably think up another thousand. We're desperate to maintain honour though and show some of that Pure Geordie Hospitality we'd so blithely promised. Jackie will not be swayed, she wants to whisk her young protege back off to London, back to civilisation.

"Could you guys call me a cab?"

"Phwoaar, it'll be expensive, that like Jackie."

"I don't care about expenses, I've just got to get Robert on that plane."

We all look at Robert – the artist – in repose, dreaming soulful visionary dreams. We call a cab. A mutually embarrassed silence descends. The taxi driver comes quick to the rescue. We wake Robert up and we troop outside, the four of us, hands are shook, a few business cards are exchanged, half-hearted exhortations to look one another up. If ever, in the area. Robert's two boxes of records are transferred from the boot of the Volvo to the boot of a Ford Siesta.

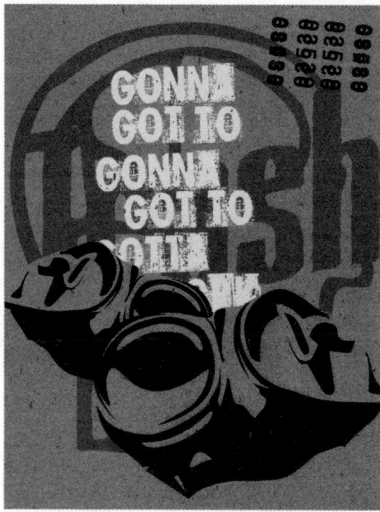

We know the taxi driver from school. He looks at us strangely. We make sure they're safely in the back of the car, make sure Robert's wearing his seat belt. It's treacherous the A18. Or whatever road it is that leads out of the Tyne Tunnel.

"And remember Jackie, if you ever want a good fireplace or any other piece of architecturals; I'm your man. I'll give you a good price."

We wave them off. Dawn is coming up. We can hear the surf lapping at the shore of King Eddie's Bay, a grey mist is hanging over the priory. It looks beautiful, to me, anyway. I've got an irrational love for the place – but then it is my hometown – even if I moved away a long time ago. Chess can't see the attraction.

"It's just a bit of owld rubble and the sea battering the sand, I can't see the attraction meself, still as long as we put on a good show for Robert and Jackie there."

We look at each other and both shrug. They'll probably miss the flight anyway, they've only got fifteen minutes.

"Especially with that fucker driving, remember him?"

"Oh aye."

We step back into the hall, step gingerly once more over the booze ridden corpse. We pug up on a bed with mates we've known from way back and crack on in that post-pill pre-pub manner. The London punters are still in the front room, dancing away oblivious, having a good time. Not such a bad party really, just the turn out let everyone down. Later we'll have breakfast, go to the Queens and take the London bods to Surfers, where DJ Conas turns in a blinding brilliant set. Surfers will be empty too but the Londoners have a great time all the same, probably something to do with the ambience of the place. (Shabby, dirty, dangerous, toytown gangster ridden womblike heaven). And not such a bad run of events in the end. The London bods are happy. Hands have been shook, connections made. The word will filter down south that John's a great host, great guy. The Res will move to Scotland. DJ Conas got to play and me and Chess happened to meet Bobby Owens. Our paths will never cross again but things like that don't matter; we still play his records and they still strike a certain chord in the soul.

Right now though we're just snuggled up on the bed. Chilling in the true sense of the word.

"By the way, who's the booze-ridden corpse in the passage?"

"Fucked if I know, some gatecrasher."

"There's always one isn't there?"

"Aye, one is all it takes."

"Aye you only need one knacker to ruin the party, I bet John wasn't too pleased."

John Fairs emerges from his room, blinking, bleary eyed.

"Has anyone seen Robert Owens?"

"Aye, Bobby, Bobby Owens he had to go, he's long gone."

He looks worried.

"Did he have a good time? Did you look after him? Did Jackie say anything?"

"What, did you mean, did we show them Pure Geordie Hospitality?"

"Yeah."

John pauses for a moment

"He definitely got Pure Geordie Hospitality?"

"When he was awake, aye."

John leaves the room to go and check on the other London Bods.

"What the fuck's he talking about Pure Geordie Hospitality?" says some cynic from a langorous position on the bed.

"Eh?"

"What the fuck's he talking about Pure Geordie Hospitality? HE'S NOT EVEN FROM NEWCASTLE."

"Course he is."

"Is he fuck, he was born in Leeds or somewhere daft."

"Aye, but he lives here."

"Aye, but he wasn't born here, he's not a true Geordie."

"Ah no, that's all we need Geordie pedantics at this time of morning."

His mate Hudson speaks up for him.

"Hey man, he's alright Fairsy."

"Nah he's not, he's a twat, gannin' on about pure Geordies and then banning his mates, how can you trust a fucker like that?"

Fuck it all, I close my eyes and drift off. These are happy days and there's some good shit going off. The Resurrection for one. Fair play to John Fairs. Some people want to get on, some want to sit back and bitch, there's always conflict of interest going on somewhere. It's just a shame there weren't any nice girls at the party, still I'll be in the pub in a few hours and besides, I've just met Robert fucking Owens. I mean it's no big deal, but it's not that bad either. Bob's

SICNOTES

O LUCKY MAN (1973)

O Lucky Man is the second part of self-proclaimed 'anarchist' Lindsay Anderson's trilogy which began with *If* (1968) and ended with *Britannia Hospital* (1982).

Clocking in at an epic three hours plus it is the twisted odyssean rise and fall and rise of Imperial Coffee salesman Mick Travis (Malcolm McDowell). Based on a story idea by McDowell, who himself had worked in the lower echelons of coffee sales, Anderson and regular screenwriting partner Sherwin take a coffee cream chocolate stuffed with razor blades to the inner workings of a multinational corporation and its many tentacled dealings, whilst maintaining a blacker than the blackest coffee coloured comedy throughout. Moreover McDowell's portrayal of Travis as a combination of innocence and optimism beyond the call of duty, and the wealth of supporting roles from the finest contemporary British character actors make it a far more savage piece than *If*. The soundtrack by Alan Price (who

also features in the film as part of a band on the road who pick Travis up when he hitches a ride) is similarly underrated, yet remarkable in its own right. All this and a twenty eight year old Helen Mirren.

In one sense it is the only British road movie of any note, overcoming the fact that the British road system will never have that vast spacious quality to support a genuine 'road movie,' by taking the back roads into the imagination. It is words drift round in my consciousnes.

GU GU GU GOTTA

GOTTA WORK

GONNA WORK

Yep if you want things to happen in this life be it spiritual, soulful, financial or whatever, you got to work at them, and that's the bottom line. I don't know why I've just written this mad story. Well I do. I wanted to pay homage to Bobby Owens really, the rest of the story is just mad dealings and if not warped with time then probably just imagined by me so it's of no real consequence. Robert standing there singing and the impact his voice had on us at that time is real though. A mate had exhorted me to go and buy a book by Roland Barthes entitled *A Discourse On Love.*

"It'll do your head in," was what he said. So there I was in the megastore on Oxford Street looking through the books. My head was in a pretty done-in state anyway and I ended up buying a copy of Bez's autobiography *Freaky Dancing* thinking that it would be a better read and knowing that it's from the maddest of the mad characters that you generally learn things anyway and at least I'd get a laugh out of Bez. It was definitely a laugh and not love that I was after. I tell you I'm sick of my life at this moment in time. My love life is a fuck-up and no mistake. I'm perpetrating shit and I know it, shit that just perpetuates, over and over. The last thing I want is some post-modern philosopher intellectualising it for me. What I want is empathy. What I need is some mad urban blues. I'm feeling a bit guilty though, thinking I'm taking the easy option in Bez over Barthes. Fuck it, I'll buy meself a record. Mr C has brought out a whole collection of Techno-y house records and I'm flicking through them when I come across the collaboration he did with Robert Owens. It's entitled A THING CALLED LOVE.

Not quite *A Discourse On Love.* But it's Bob and that's enough for me.

It's a long time since he brought out a record and a mutual friend who was there at the time said Mr C was in a pretty psychotropic state of mind when he produced the session. I'm always up for anything adventurous and renegade... ✖

the flip side of *It's A Wonderful Life* and what the Coen brothers' *Hudsucker Proxy* might have been.

Anderson pulls no punches, slipping in real footage of a third world coffee production line and showing film of Vietnamese napalm victims 'which comes overlaid with a cold, dispassionate discussion about market feasibility and the suppression of rebel forces, (and) succeeds in hitting a blackness that is almost unwatchable' (Richard Scheib).

There is a laugh-out-loud scene in it which sticks in my mind. Travis is on trial having been set up as a fall guy, and the elderly, sour-faced judge retires to his Chambers at a critical stage, for some moments to deliberate. Cut to the inside of the Chambers. Accompanied by the court clerk, the judge casually slips off his robes and is dressed only in socks and shoes, a red satin thong and with his legal wig still on his head. Without any fuss he lies face down on the table and the clerk administers several swift lashes with a serious cane across his back. He gets dressed again and walks back into court. It is the lightest of moments yet captures the dark side of authority, which runs throughout the film and through society then and now.

It's not that we begrudge the judge getting off on being caned, if he so desires; rather we know that he will deny it thrice and thrice again in public, and because he represents authority which punishes any and every transgression if it is practised by the non-privileged classes.

Aye and there's the rub. Anderson's trilogy is a remarkable exploration of class war, not seen before or since on the silver screen, and delivers a riotous assembly of revolutionary intent which hits the mark with savage humour and necessary rancour, yet never fails to be entertaining.
Danbert Nobacon

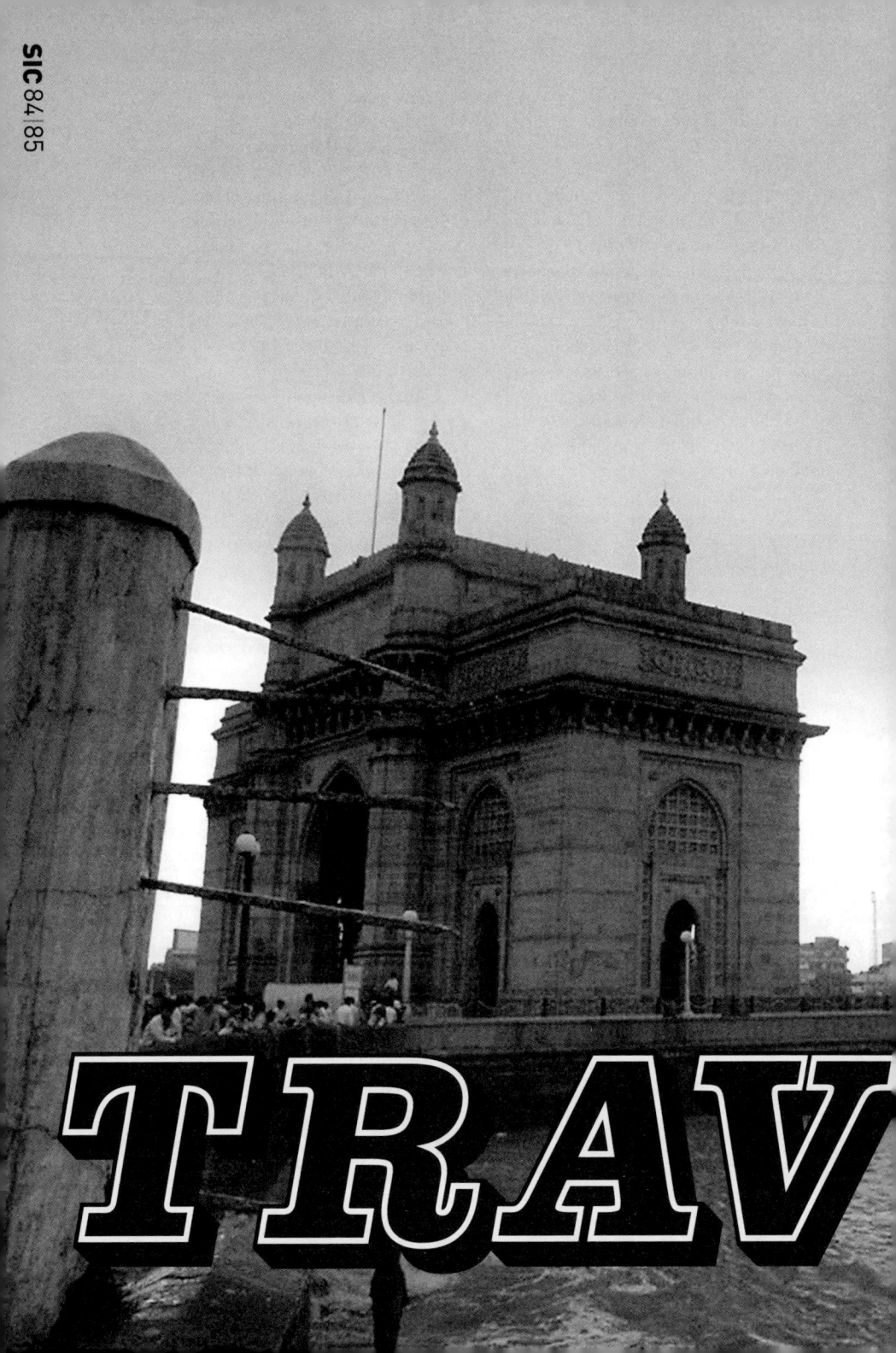

TRAV

Join *Sic* as we take a flying leap into the global village – no cheap flights, holidays in hell or trips off the beaten track. *Sic* heads straight for the eye of the storm…

"DON'T SHOOT – I'M BRITISH!"

Jeremy Hardy packs his Ambre Solaire and heads off to Palestine

I admit that I despair slightly when I hear British people and Palestinian exiles extolling the heroism of the fighters, saying how inspiring the struggle is, how it will prevail or be a 'fight to the death'. The Tanzim have rifles. They are up against tanks and helicopter gunships, deployed by a militarised state that is bankrolled and armed by the most powerful country on earth. The Palestinians inspire me because they are human, and humanity inspires me.

I wince when I see the slogan 'Victory to the Intifada!' below a picture of a youth with a sling-shot. That youth is almost certainly dead now. You can be as inspired by him as you like; it won't help him.

This sounds very cynical but it's not meant to. If I learned anything in Palestine it was to be more self-critical and less judgmental. So, here is my story.

In February, I was approached by the Palestinian film-maker, Leila Sansour, to present a documentary about the International Solidarity Movement in Palestine. The group is based in Beit Sahour, near Bethlehem, and it brings activists from around the world to witness and oppose the Israeli occupation of the lands seized in 1967.

In principle, the ISM defends the right of Palestinians to resist the occupation. It opposes attacks on civilians but there are differing opinions within it about the use of guerrilla tactics against the army. Some of the organisers hope that non-violent resistance might replace the armed struggle, and there are very practical arguments that support this view. Palestinian fighters are hopelessly outgunned by one of the most powerful armies in the world. On Good Friday, I flew out of Heathrow on El Al. It was an early flight, otherwise I would have heard the news that Ariel Sharon intended to invade the whole of the West Bank. It's quite likely that I would then have decided the trip was sheer madness. I was already extremely wary and had promised my daughter that I'd be very careful; and I wasn't sure that being careful was compatible with going at all.

In any event, I fetched up at Heathrow and joined the check-in queue for El Al, which involves questions about the nature of one's trip and a complete search of all luggage. I was told by the security people that it would be much better to give my hand luggage to them so it could be given back to me at the boarding gate and it wouldn't have to be searched again on the way into Departures. At the gate, it became clear that not everyone had been advised thus, and that those of us who had would face a final body search before getting our hand luggage back. The passing of a metal detector over the soles of my shoes revealed a drawing pin, which was kindly removed.

On arrival at Ben Gurion airport, there were more questions about the purpose of my trip. I mumbled things about being a writer interested in life in the Palestinian Territories, which didn't endear me but didn't seem to worry

them too much. At Arrivals, I met Nicholas Blincoe, a writer married to Leila, with several of the ISM activists: Rory MacMillan, a lawyer, Emma Bleach, a student, Jo Bird who works for the Co-op, Chris Dunham, an energy consultant and Kunle Ibidun who does something with mobile phones. Jo, Chris and Kunle had met at university and were veterans of a previous ISM fortnight. The ISM organises three big trips a year, although it is now desperate to get people to go whenever they can.

After a long delay at the Bethlehem checkpoint, with soldiers peering into the car again and again as though they might find different people in it each time, we were waved through, and after a few minutes arrived at the Star Hotel. We new arrivals signed in, had a couple of drinks and then joined the rest of the group (about seventy in all) for dinner and a meeting to welcome us. The new arrivals were then asked to try and form 'affinity groups'. I was uncertain about this structure, feeling that dividing us into small groups might be a way of controlling us. Personally, I am happy to speak up and argue in a large meeting, although I came to appreciate that quieter people are more confident among a group of six or seven. Each affinity group chooses a spokesperson who gathers the feelings of the group. All the spokespeople then meet as a spokes-council with organisers. There are sometimes differences among people as to what should be discussed in affinity groups and what should be aired in a larger meeting but the structure seems to work and no-one gets sidelined or marginalised.

Newcomers to the movement have to go through a morning of non-violence training, which is essential for one's own safety apart from anything else. We were facing a level of state violence much higher than most of us were used to. It was vital that we did not allow ourselves to be panicked or provoked. On previous trips, activists had faced verbal and physical abuse from settlers, tear gas and percussion grenades from police and soldiers. The 'rubber bullets' used are real bullets with a rubber coating and army, police and settlers are all heavily armed. As it turned out, we saw no settlers or police; we were to see an invasion.

But the non-violence training was interesting. It was still my first full day and I was getting into the swing of things. The training was given by the Christian Peacemaker Team, who gave us other useful bits of advice on how to behave. One thing that I tried to hold on to was 'Don't steal the show'. So often in any human interaction we are so busy thinking about what we are about to say that we forget to listen. And we all have a tendency to tell others what they should do or what our experiences have been, when they just want to tell their story. It takes a lot of drive to be an activist, and it's hard to be driven and humble.

We were also prepared for the likelihood of arrest and it was impressed upon us that we should try to interpose ourselves to prevent the arrest of Palestinians, and if necessary get arrested along with them. Perhaps the most important role of the ISM activist is to lessen the oppression of Palestinians by being prepared to bear witness to it. To this end, many activists spend some or all of their time in refugee camps.

I intended to do this at the end of the first day, but Leila asked me to stay at the hotel because she needed me early in the morning to go and film interviews. In the morning, Leila picked me up and we rushed down to meet the Mayor, Hanna Nasser, at the Church of the Nativity. This was to be my potted tour of Bethlehem: the Church of the Nativity, followed by a house shelled from an Israeli army base, followed by the maternity hospital and Dheisha Refugee camp.

Then Leila took me to a lunch party she'd organised with some of her relatives so I could hear how some of the more comfortably off Palestinians feel about the situation. Their views were varied and interesting, but, after my visit to the maternity hospital, I couldn't string a coherent sentence together. I had seen the intensive care unit where the blast from a shell showered the incubators with glass two years ago, and damage done when a tank pulled up outside in October and sprayed the front of the hospital with bullets. The focus of the attack appears to have been the statue of the Virgin Mary, who took dozens of bullets. She didn't fall, so the army fired a wire guided missile at her. I found myself shocked but laughing. I know that her statues are reputed to move, but did the Israeli Defence Force see her reaching for a concealed device?

None of the women or children were hurt in the hospital on that occasion but a woman held at a checkpoint on her way to give birth, had her baby in front of the army with no assistance and the child died. Half the beds are empty because the women are simply stopped at checkpoints.

It was clear that we were not talking about nervous young soldiers panicking. The occupation is brutal and the aim is to crush Palestine. Increasing numbers of Israeli soldiers are refusing to serve in the Occupied Territories for this reason. It is not that they are scared. The Palestinian fighters have rifles, the IDF has tanks and Apache helicopters.

Moreover, a man I had met in the camp and all of the people at lunch had told me that our being internationals would make no difference to the army, and that it was quite likely that we would be killed. I was now very jumpy. I was thinking the whole ISM strategy was crazy, that activists would be asleep in the camps as the IDF fired shells into them. I'd been told in Dheisha that, if the IDF tried to enter the camp, they

would meet armed resistance. This would be the cue for tanks and bulldozers. I now thought that activists provided a great morale boost to the locals, but absolutely no protection. Indeed, I thought many would be killed. And I thought they were perhaps crazy, naïve, manipulable or vainglorious, wanting a story to brag about when they got home.

The next morning there was a meeting of the whole group in the hotel and a couple of people expressed concerns about the situation we were in. This was my cue to let rip. To my shame, I gave vent to my view that to imagine we offered any kind of protection to the Palestinians was naïve. Later having let off steam, I regretted my outburst. I had demoralised people, undervalued them and undermined the organisation. Nonetheless, that night, most of them went back into the camps, and I believe by their presence saved the lives of many Palestinians.

After the meeting, I made peace with a number of people. They were a very forgiving group and realised much more clearly than I did that I had just lost it. I had also been the catalyst for a

1977. Me? Suburban schoolboy billy-no-mates virgin twat.

Them? Skinny, sullen Apollonian mod gods. Instant shell-shock.

Splintered, paint-spattered and battered-guitar-twatting Oxfam-clobbered cock-stiffening'n' cunt-drenching ugly-pretty boy über-yobs with dog eyes, sex hair and the thin twitching limbs of smackfucked'n' tapewormriddled ultramodels.

Day-glo homocommie kneetrembler chic.

Fuck! Glottal-stop mock-cockernee agit-prop retro-pop punk rock.

FUCK! Chunka chunka, reggae style drop-out. Rapid strobe rock. THAT glottal-stop gobbed sulphate stammer. Flickering shutter rock. Speed stuttering. Absolute total never-ever-to-be-touched-ever-again numb-tongued ning-nang-nong nirvana. So stiffly male, so limply butch. So CARNIVOROUS. So effortlessly, cockthrobbingly, cunt-drenchingly, nippletwitchingly, mindblowingly, punk-rockingingly absolutely fucking aesthetically and politically flawed AND totally perfect. THE CLASH.

Perspective? Fuck you, anarcho finger-sniffer. Tick off all their faults, list all their failures, mention at length all their fuck-ups and mistakes and you're still left with the much greater reality of the rock'n'roll band who re-defined rock'n'roll as a culture of protest, riot, rage and liberation.

That attitude. That aesthetic. That agenda.

The story is the Manic Street Preachers – a bunch of brilliant, utterly fucked off, self-educated working class kids in South Wales in the 1980s – coming across the

discussion that dispersed some of the tension and clarified what we there for. So I like to think that by being wrong I served a purpose. But I think I was just wrong and I still wince when I think about it.

However, there was a march to Beit Jala and I wanted to take part. Beit Jala

had already been invaded and the aim was to show solidarity with the people there. The weather was warming up and we joined with some very cheerful Italian activists so spirits rose as we marched the short distance.

We were about to become an international incident. We followed our

Clash and thinking FUCK!

It's the story of Tim from Rancid – a fucked up alcoholic Californian skate punk in the 1990s – who hammers a punk band together because he can't get the clanging chords of 'Remote Control' out of his spiky head,

The story is how a self-regarding, cliquey little London art-school take on New York underground rock became the last great (and genuinely populist) mass art movement of the 20th century. How nihilism became revolution. How elitism became empowerment. How it made revolutionary socialism

racial miscegenation and righteous anti-fascism into pop phenomena. How it made rock stars out of its audience

The story is about how a bunch of scruffed-up, fucked-up and sulphate-scrambled ex-skinheads, proto-mods, secret poshoes, wannabe guitar heroes and pup pub-rockers sold themselves (and got sold) as Che Guevara with attack guitars.

The story is Lewisham and Victoria Park and that Sounds first cover. Of Rock Against Racism, The Anti-Nazi League and a million children refusing the role society has planned for

them.

A set of ideas. A set of possibilities. Yep, buy the boxed set, watch the videos, just consume if you want. But the template – the idea that the band as a gang, the band as an on-stage riot, as flawed gurus, the band as guerrillas, the band as propagandists, the band as revolutionaries, rabble-rousers, rebel rockers – makes all the other proffered alternatives look lame, weak, pasty-faced and pitiful by comparison.

Stephen Wells

non-violence training, stopping some yards short of an armoured personnel carrier, falling silent and keeping still. Two people chosen as negotiators, Kunle and Lillian Pizzichini, a journalist from London, approached with arms outstretched to see if we might be allowed to pass. Without warning, shots were fired, some into the cobblestones and some straight at us. Kunle was hit in three places by shrapnel and an Australian woman called Kate took a direct hit in the stomach. But they kept firing. People had their hands in the air and backed calmly away but still the shooting continued. Several protestors were hit. Then the media were shot at. A Palestinian reporter was saved by his flak jacket.

But still, that night, most of the group volunteered to go into the three camps. By now, it was clear that an invasion was hours away. Those who stayed in the hotel reacted in different ways, some taking names and passport numbers and ringing embassies; some of us drinking the bar dry while trying to give articulate interviews to the media. By the morning, we were in a movie: gunfire raging, tanks outside the windows, journalists everywhere, curtains closed, people crouching on floors trying to give not the slightest excuse to the IDF. One Italian reporter took a peek out of an upstairs window and was shot at.

Kunle had asked the consulate to try to get him out. His father had died at about the same time as he was being shot and he needed to get back to be with his mother. Over the next few hours, several more us decided to go with him.

We were all worried about what we were putting our families through, and our main use to the Palestinians was in contacting the media, something we could do much more easily back in England.

It was two days before the consulate were allowed through the checkpoint. We spent the whole time giving phone interviews, not to tell our story, but because down the road the IDF was firing bullets and shells into people's homes. So far, the presence of internationals in the camps was working, but we didn't know for how long.

We were holed-up but fairly safe. Not far away, there were bodies in streets and in houses, and hundreds of people had taken refuge in churches – fighters and civilians alike. Armed resistance faces hopeless odds and offers the IDF an excuse for atrocities, but the occupying troops need little provocation and most civilians see the fighters as their defenders.

On Wednesday, a convoy arrived. Bullet-proof cars from the British, American and Japanese consulates pulled up with an IDF escort. It felt odd having protection from Israeli soldiers, but it guaranteed that their colleagues wouldn't shoot us. An hour later the British consul and his wife were giving us gin and tonics and spaghetti bolognese. We all felt a mixture of emotions: relief, a desperate urge to get home and quite a lot of guilt about leaving.

Some of the people we left in the hotel stayed for weeks. Rory was to go on to Jenin. Mary Kelly, an Irish nurse, stayed for two months and was one of the people who later snuck into the Church of the Nativity, stayed there until seized by the army ten days later, then spent four days in jail before being deported.

I saw Mary in London on her way home. She told me how frightened she had been in those first few days when I'd got to know her. I think everyone was frightened. Certainly anyone with any sense and who enjoys living. Courage isn't the absence of fear or a delight in danger; courage lies in overcoming fear for a purpose.

The activists I met were an extraordinarily diverse bunch, from all over the world and from all sorts of political, social and ethnic backgrounds, teenagers and pensioners, black and white, Asian and Jewish. They had differing ideas, even about the situation we were in. But they were all prepared to listen to and respect each other because they were there for a common purpose. They were all brave and they made me certain of the goodness in the human heart. Some were prickly and had an infuriating tendency to dismiss the mainstream media as though it exists in another dimension. My view is that Indymedia is fantastic but if you can get on *Richard and Judy*, do it.

Some people were as suspicious of me as I was of them, but I like to think that some became as fond of me as I became of them. Sometimes I wondered what we were doing there and thought we were revolutionary tourists who would go back to our lives to hold court

about our brush with death; that we could come and go and the Palestinians couldn't.

Bizarrely perhaps, but for that very reason, I found the courage of the activists had a greater effect on me than that of the Palestinians. What impressed me most about the local people was the thing that has struck me about all people forced into extraordinary situations: how ordinary they are, and how they are more worried about others than about themselves. They have an extraordinary tale to tell but they are concerned about whether you've eaten.

"What impressed me most about the Palestinians was the thing that has struck me about all people forced into extraordinary situations: how ordinary they are"

In national liberation politics, the left so often wants heroes and iconography, and we get seduced by the sexiness of it all. Supporting an armed struggle gives us an automatic militancy and entry into what feels like 'where it's happening'. In fact, armed struggle can involve no politics at all. When one is focused on the struggle, the kind of national homeland one is fighting for is secondary. Ideology or faith are very often bolted-on to be dispensed with

THE CONTINUUM CONCEPT

by Jean Liedloff

This is one of those books which when I read it, gives me a physical experience of expanding consciousness – and I can physically feel my heart sinking as it leads to realisation of what we are doing to ourselves. It's primarily about how we treat children but it has other insights into how we are as human beings and gives some steps towards creating a more human-friendly society.

Jean Liedloff lived with a stone age Indian tribe in the South American jungle for over two years. It was an enlightening experience for her. As she puts it, "I would be ashamed to admit to the Indians that where I come from the women do not feel themselves capable of raising children until they read the instructions written in a book by a strange man." Her basic conclusion was that the current period of 'civilisation' – which has lasted only a few thousand years – directly contradicts much of the experience and expectations arising from millions of years of human history prior to this time. The intellect, she says, has triumphed over innate characteristics: and many of these innate characteristics provide the conditions for human beings together being happy and being fulfilled.

The book does not at all suggest any return to stone age society but it proposes analysis of many of the social ills and problems present in civilised society. At a time of such apparent prosperity (at least in the developed world), in reality many of us are left with feelings of emptiness, disconnection and despair – which is expressed through depression, addictive behaviour, self-destructive patterns and lack of respect for others. But it has not always been so and it does not have to be so. And that's one reason why you are reading this magazine: because you/I/we believe that there can be more to life than this.

Jean Liedloff says that when born, babies need the constant physical presence of their mother and that for the first period of life, the mother is a passive figure while the baby is an active participant. So the baby demands and gets food, the baby demands and gets affection – when the baby needs it. This sets the foundations for the baby believing that he or she is inherently lovable. This has been the baby's sense in the womb and it is necessary to firmly establish this for the first months after birth. To quote, "lovableness is the basic feeling about self that is appropriate to the individuals of our species. Without the sense of being lovable, one has no sense of how much one ought to claim of comfort, security, help, companionship, love, friendship, things, pleasure or joy." Added to this lovableness is the constant stimulation which comes from simply being around other people, both adults and children.

From this stage, the baby looks forwards and outwards to the world, exploring it with eagerness – and this eagerness develops strong self-reliance and evolves his or her innate sociability. The key at this stage from the parents is guidance as opposed to curbing because "it is assumed that the child is social, not anti-social in his motives."

The child is able to take care of his or herself, the child does not have inherently suicidal tendencies – in fact, it is the opposite. The child has inherent tendencies of self-preservation and a desire to interact with other human beings, to be part of human society.

But civilisation has created conditions where "happiness ceases to be a normal condition of being alive and becomes a goal." And so we start living in the past, the future, anywhere but the moment of now. Our lives are a list of 'if-only' and we survive rather than live, with our fundamental need for love being hijacked by, for example, adverts with their claims of 'the real thing'.

A sense of rightness, being centred and at peace in the actual moment, is a rare experience for virtually all of us. For it to come about, we need to reconnect with our innate tendencies and use the intellect as a servant rather than a master – for it is an incompetent and unhappy master. Techniques such as meditation (and other methods where we go deep inside ourselves) can help. And – of course – radical restructuring of society. To be able to bring up children along some of these lines requires such a restructuring – but without some of these changes happening now, such a restructuring is in all probability doomed to failure, recreating the old patterns. There needs to be a constant dynamic between changes in the here and now and creating conditions for broader changes in social relationships (that might be called a revolution but remember that a successful revolution is virtually all evolution).

There can be – obviously – criticisms made of this book. Jean Liedloff has herself amended some slight sections on her website (particularly those relating to sexuality – the book was written in 1975). There are dangers in transferring observations about one culture to another that is very different (although we both walk upright, speak, socialise, build houses, have sex, laugh, play). And there are also dangers in people becoming 'guilty' about some of the proposals – 'I'm a bad parent because I'm not doing this or that.' Guilt – like worry – serves no purpose at all.

We all need to take responsibility for our lives, understand the direct connection between actions and consequences and be happy. Personally, I don't have children so that might be a criticism levelled at me: writing a review of a book about bringing up children. But this book is about much more than bringing up children, it's about how we live and who we are, subjects that at heart interest all of us. It is definitely worth reading – and then starting to put some of the ideas into practice.

Norman

later, just as faiths and ideologies bolt on liberation struggles to accessorise their own strategies.

I was afraid I would witness the kind of nationalism-worship the left has so often engaged in before. Sometimes we choose our country, buy the t-shirt and then extol the culture as though that's the point. People adopted Cuba, Nicaragua, Ireland (less so as it was too close for comfort), Palestine or black Africa and immersed themselves in adoration. Of course, cultures need to rescue themselves when the oppressor has cast them as non-existent or savage, but the fight for justice shouldn't be a beauty contest.

The fact is the Palestinians are just human beings, and human beings will fight back, especially when they have no choice. No nation, race or culture has a monopoly on bravery or dignity. Throughout the world and throughout history we can see people who have very little but will share it, people who smile in the face of adversity and people who will fight and die for a principle. Many people observe that Palestinians are warm and hospitable people and Israelis rude and aggressive and there is some truth in those stereotypes. But unless you believe it's genetic, you must conclude that we tend to behave in a way determined by the roles in which we are cast.

I met no-one among the activists who was intoxicated with Arab nationalism or saw this as the struggle of a proud people whose case is based on the beauty of their headscarves. The ISM is organised by Palestinians and that is important because activists must put themselves at their service. But it is a truly internationalist movement that reflects the changes in the way we do politics. The activists are part of the struggle to be human, wherever that takes them. ✖

The return of the tortoise

Sic **looks to Italy and sees a movement catching history on the wing**

Two thousand or so years ago the Imperial Roman army invented a tactic called the tortoise where a group of soldiers combined their shields to form a shell. This military formation was almost invincible, the tortoise could advance forwards, protected from attack, and with its collective armour it outmanoeuvred the barbarians who fought as individuals. The tortoise played a part in enabling Rome to become an empire straddling the Ancient world, smashing all resistance and swallowing every society it encountered. Now a new empire is emerging, a global empire which engulfs everything it comes across and destroys or soaks up all resistance. In the late 1990s the tortoise re-emerged; its strength was still social co-operation but this time its ethos was anti-Empire.

October 24th 1998 was a European-wide day of protest against the death of Semira Adamu, a Nigerian girl killed by the Belgian police. In Italy there was a demonstration against an immigrant detention centre in Trieste. The Trieste demonstrators looked different from the usual raggle-taggle of political t-shirts and sensible boots; they wore white overalls with home-made foam and cardboard body armour beneath. Their comical roly-poly appearance belied the fact that they were deadly serious. The white overalls on the front lines had crash helmets and home-made Plexiglas shields. To the amazement of the police the shield-bearers started to group together, a line of chalky white demonstrators overlapping their shields, the rows behind raising their shields above their heads as protection from rubber bullets and tear gas. The demonstration was attacked by police and customs officers, but the front-line was able to resist and advance to the fences of the detention camp. There, after hours of alternate clashes and negotiations, a number of people were allowed to enter the camp for the first time and document the inhuman conditions of the prisoners. A month later on the 15th November the camp was closed. The tortoise had re-emerged out of history.

1977

How did this happen? Why did such a bizarre and innovative form of protest resurface? It wasn't because the demonstrators had watched *Spartacus* over and over again; the tactics of the white overalls (Tute Bianche) were the result of ten years of theoretical and political development, a decade which saw the Italian movement become the largest and most vibrant in Europe. Italy's political progress was highlighted by the size and intensity of the protests

Movement of '77

against the G8 in Genoa in 2001 and by the horrific violence used to repress those demonstrations.

The tortoise's head

The use of shields and padding by the Italian movement captured the imagination of the anti-globalisation movement. Padded armour disrupted the distinction between violence and non-violence, confounding the mass media which tried to divide protesters into good and bad. Being padded, the demonstrators could achieve their aims without having to fight the police on the police's terms. Though they threw the police and the media off-balance the Tute

Bianche's actions haven't always been understood by activists from other countries, and their methods have led to allegations of elitism or pacifism. To understand the Tute Bianche we have to look at what has happened to the Italian left over the last thirty years – the roots of today's tactics lie in that experience.

In 1977 while Britain was rocked by the Summer of Punk, Italy was experiencing social upheaval on an altogether grander scale. Unlike the rest of Europe, the revolutionary fervour of 1968 didn't come to an abrupt end in Italy, but continued to develop for another decade. A cycle of struggles autonomous from the large Italian Communist Party reached its high point with a series of massive demonstrations based around university and workplace occupations. These events – which came to be known as the 'Movement of 77' – were an explosion of creative energy which sparked new sensibilities and experimental ways of living. Young people no longer had the same desires as their parents: the jobs for life that the previous generation had fought for now represented a prison of interminable boredom. This generation saw work as an unpleasant chore to be endured, now and then, to finance what they really wanted to do.

In the time

liberated from work, young people squatted social centres, they set up free radio stations and set about self-reducing the cost of living through campaigns to make goods and services a token 'political price'. The movement was playful and ironic, pricking the usual pomposity of Italian politics. Protesters turned up at demonstrations dressed as American Indians with painted faces and feathers in their hair, and continued the theme by signing political communiqués 'Apache' or 'Mr. Tomahawk'. The press quickly dubbed them the 'Metropolitan Indians'. Despite this playfulness large sections of the movement weren't against the use of force – the left often had to defend itself

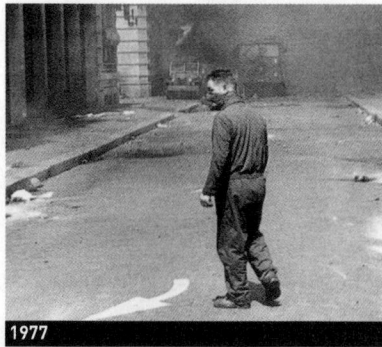

1977

SICNOTES

When I was 16 I got a summer job in a chemical factory near to my home in Glasgow. I was off to university in September so it was temporary, but it was useful getting some cash for the summer.

I worked with the men, putting great big barrels of chemicals into enormous vats to make cleaning stuff or disinfectant or whatever. The women would bottle the stuff coming out the vats and stick labels on the bottles. Sometimes totally different labels would go on stuff from the same vat – there would be a cheap label and some fancy label that cost loads more. Same stuff though.

It was pretty disgusting work, but you could have a laugh. Sometimes we'd just sit

around after filling a vat while the women did the assembly line thing. Sometimes the women would tell us to hurry up if they were getting bored of hanging around waiting on us to get a vat ready. Being the newest and youngest, and the smarty-pants college kid, I got sent to the other end of the factory sometimes for a long stand or some tartan paint. The gaffer there would just growl and send me back.

The company was run by a lord, a Labour Party lord. He had a Rolls Royce that he got chauffeured to work in. There was an office up the top and everyone said that he just went up there and drank whisky all day when he was in, which wasn't that often as I remember.

Anyway, one day the word

goes around that we're on strike. I didn't really get this because there wasn't any build-up, no-one had been complaining or anything, it just seemed weird. Then someone explained that it wasn't a real strike. We just stopped work for the afternoon once a year while our union official went up to sort a pay deal with the boss in his office. He'd gone up there already and we all walked out for a while until he came down and told us what he'd got.

Sounded all right to me. It was quite a sunny day and everyone just sat out in the yard. After a while, this union official came down, looking a bit pissed, gathered everyone together and started to speak.

To be honest, I can't remember much of what he said. It was very emotional against fascist groups and the violence of the state. Nor did the movement feel it had to stay within the law: tactics for reducing prices included mass looting sprees which were dubbed 'proletarian shopping'.

The 'Movement of 77' reached its high-water mark in March when huge demonstrations – sparked by the police killing an activist – seized large parts of Rome and Bologna and held them for ten days. In Rome a gun shop was looted and the guns thrown away. This was a clear pronouncement to the state: "We can get guns if we are forced to." In Bologna there were armoured cars on the streets and mass arrests. Against a background of increasing violence from the police and fascist groups, and the emergence of clandestine armed groups in response to these attacks, the movement found itself forced off the creative terrain it had carved out. Suddenly it was locked into a fight it couldn't win. Trapped in a deadly

1977

spiralling embrace with the state, the time and space for creativity closed up. In Italy the 1970s ended with state repression unprecedented in post-war Western Europe. The clampdown left hundreds of militants dead and thousands in prison. The movement was crushed, leaving a legacy of defeat, disillusion and a heroin epidemic.

The trauma of the late 1970s had a lasting effect on the next generation of militants. The use of protected

though, he'd been fighting for us and he'd got us a great deal. The main thing about this deal was how the women got a bigger percentage increase than the men, he went on and on about this and the women, who were about two thirds of the workers, loved it. They got paid less than the men and this was something that was going to help sort that out. The union man called a quick vote and all the women voted for the deal, making faces at the men. The men complained but the union man said "That's the vote" and went back inside with the lord.

It took about twenty minutes for people to work out we'd been stitched up. The difference the women were getting above the men was pretty tiny and didn't give them equal pay or anything – and both wage rises

were well below inflation. People sort of knew this all along, but it was as if there was nothing we could do about it. People kept saying, "The T & G steward sorts it out, he knows what he's doing." There wasn't any bitterness between the men and women, more a feeling that that was just life. And that there wasn't a lot you could do about it.

I didn't learn that women are gullible or workers are suckers from that strike. I remembered how well that union man worked the crowd, using his fiery rhetoric so it seemed impossible to argue with him. And I learnt how, when things get going, those with power will always find plausible people to keep things safe for them until things go quiet again.

I went on to university and never had to work in a chemical factory again. But I remember that set-up, the Labour lord and his union pal stitching everyone up, while pretending to be on our side. I've seen it loads since then – Paul Boateng during the Brixton uprisings telling the black youth to trust him because he was their friend, Bill Morris promising the Liverpool dockers his full backing, Communist Party (and more recently SWP) stewards on marches telling people to stay in line and not cause a scene because everything's being taken care of.

And every time they do, I remember that union man telling us pretty much the same thing before going back in for another whisky with the lord.
Colin Chalmers

demonstrations has to be seen in this light. The padding was a practical and creative attempt to scale down the violence of the forces of law and order. Italian activists had learned valuable lessons from the repression.

What remained of the movement in the 1980s regrouped around squatted social centres and a few remaining free radio stations. They reflected the more creative side of the 'Movement of 77', allowing a new strategy of exodus. The movement avoided confronting the state on its own ground but sought to weaken it through defection. This strategy was potentially problematic; it could have led to isolation, a separating off from society into an inward-looking ghetto. Some called the social centres of the 1980s Indian Reservations. To some extent these problems were kept at bay with music, as long-standing Italian militant Hobo explains:

Prague, September 2000

"Music was very important in the social centres. It was a way to attract people, it provided culture and finance."

Music might have kept the torch of radicalism supplied with oxygen but it took a new wave of university occupations in 1990 to fully ignite it and break the spell of defeat. Dubbed the Panther Movement (because it coincided with the escape of a panther from Rome Zoo), the protests revitalised the movement. The protesters were brash and inventive and knew how to manipulate the media. The escaped panther seemed to symbolise the escape from blocked thinking and pessimism.

As Hobo recalls: "Panther brought a real renewal in the social centres, supplying vital energy and wiping out that diffuse sense of defeat. Many new social centres (actually, most of the existing social centres) were occupied in those years by the panther students. The panther movement marked the beginning of the longer process of de-ghettoisation."

This de-ghettoisation was aided by a journey undertaken by Italian activists into the misty jungles of southern Mexico. The Zapatista movement had burst on to the world stage with their uprising on January 1st, 1994. It sent shock waves around the globe. To some they looked like a throwback to earlier times but their politics were something new. Inventive, expansive and un-dogmatic, the Zapatistas constantly looked outwards to defend their revolution. They called an International Encuentro (encounter) in their jungle stronghold in 1996; thousands attended from every corner of the world. The Encuentro played an important part in bringing together the counter-globalisation movement that Seattle made public. In Italy they built an influential network of groups called Ya Basta (Enough). Their role was to support the Zapatistas but also to apply the new ways of thinking to the struggle in Italy. The Italians who attended took away a new attitude to politics that gelled well with their own experiences. These included:-

■ Change the world without taking power

- March with questions on your lips, not with a blueprint for revolution
- Reject the old binaries that had trapped thinking for so long: violence/non-violence, reform/revolution
- Seek a world made of differences, a world containing many worlds, a world without borders
- Many Yeses, One No – our struggles are united by our shared opposition to capitalism

Ghost town

Italy in the 1990s, like many other countries, experienced a growing disaffection with mainstream politics. The left with its newly expanded social centres didn't have the playing field all to itself. The anger and powerlessness associated with 'globalisation' was seized upon and used by opportunistic right-wing parties to gain power. In Italy the racist Lega Nord (Northern League) were quick to exploit the dissatisfaction.

As Hobo explains: "Lega Nord was successful, so we started asking why. They collected the protest and displeasure of a lot of people, channelling it into the worst populist platitudes. In most of the cases the roots of this protest were fair, but people were duped. They fed their rage with intolerance and egotism."

In fact the struggle with the Lega Nord lies at the root of the emergence of the white overall as a symbol. In 1994 the Lega Nord Mayor of Milan ordered the eviction of the oldest and largest social centre in Italy, the Leoncavallo. The mayor boasted: "From now on, squatters will be nothing more than ghosts wandering about in the city!" Protesters took this description literally: during the demonstrations to protect the Leoncavallo large numbers put on ghostly white overalls and rioted in the

Genoa, July 2001

centre of the city. The symbolism of the white overalls had a powerful resonance; it made visible those who had been ignored but it took a further rhetorical connection to launch the Tute Bianche as an Italian-wide movement.

The Italian job

In Italian the phrase tute blu (blue overall) is the equivalent of blue collar in England and America: tute blu represents the traditional manual worker. But work has changed. The introduction of information and computer technologies has made work seem more immaterial and ghostly. Work is less about making material goods and more about providing services, knowledge and culture. The emphasis is on producing changes in the way people think or feel. Even in industries producing something physical like cars, the material part seems to be less important than the intangible bits like the concept and the brand. The lifestyle the car represents has now become the pivotal point. The experience of work has changed. Jobs are more precarious and insecure, with short-term contracts, self-employment and frequent job changes. Work now seems to invade the whole of life. The distinction between work time and leisure seems to be breaking down, in an age of home computers, mobile phones, endless adverts and constant shopping we're always at work and work is never finished. It's as if the whole of society has become one giant factory.

When Italian theorists began examining the new work experience, the contrast with the tute blu was too tempting: the new marginalised workers, the unemployed and temporary workers formed the bedrock of the social centres. Tute Bianche started to be linked to the new work experiences. In November 1998 a national white overalls day was declared with demonstrations outside the stock exchange, council chambers and employment agencies. The wearing of white overalls swept through Italy with many of the Ya Basta network adopting the Tute Bianche dress and politics.

Hobo explains: "The Tute Bianche experience started from research (mainly conducted by Toni Negri and Maurizio Lazzarato) on 'immaterial work' – a new concept that helped investigate some major changes happening in society. There's been a continuous feedback between these intellectuals and the movement. The Tute Bianche struggled for the

Milan, January 2000

extension of rights to non-workers; linking the political to the social, putting bodies and lives centre stage. These times are too historically different from previous phases; we have to try new roads and constantly verify them with theory."

This new movement and thinking was brought together at a 1998 conference of social centres, where they agreed a series of proposals known as the Milan Charter. According to Hobo: "The charter talked about the need for plural participation in this mass movement, with wide and rich differences... So they proposed the creation of a network organised by Tute Bianche. The critical point was that the movement must exit the losing loop of 'conflict – repression – struggle against repression'. The aim was to enter a different scene; where social conflict can bring positiveness and start a new loop of 'conflict – projects – broadening of the sphere of rights'."

This was an attempt to break away from the margins, to bring an end to the paralysis of purity. Hands were going to get dirty but just how dirty was controversial. The charter talked of the need to get recognition of their rights in all areas of society, even in

government, though it was important to the Tute Bianches not to focus too much on the latter. In their view the state had become less powerful as it was overcome by global capitalism. It was out in wider society that the real battles were to be fought, but unfortunately the state still remained an important point of repression. The movement had to manage its relationship to the state as a means of defence. For instance sympathetic mayors and MPs were encouraged on to demonstrations to make it difficult for the media to demonise the protesters. Some of those linked to the movement even stood in local council elections, occasionally getting elected. All of this was heresy in a tradition that prided itself on its autonomy. In many ways it was an admirable refusal to be hemmed in by political orthodoxy, but the tactic had the potential to blunt the movement's opposition to hierarchy and parliamentary politics. To Hobo it was worth the risk:

"The point was: let's start from this and try to acquire some rights that can be extended overall. I can't say if this is a good strategy, I can only see the results and in my opinion they confirm the initial bet. We have been able to bring members of parliament to Belgrade and Ramallah to give voice to the movement, we have been able to bring them to detention camps for immigrants and close them... but above all, we can move from a defensive role and try to propose

what we want. We have to fight hard (and Genoa was a dramatic example) but we can't easily be pointed out as isolated thugs... even the right-wing journals are forced to refer to us as a social movement. They can talk about violence, radicalism, whatever, but they have to admit we represent a part of this society.

"Of course there wasn't complete agreement with the new flexibility. In a very schematic way, we can say that there was a part of the movement oriented towards investigating and interpreting the changes in the world – in politics, in society and in production; while there was another part tied to orthodox Marxism and to an unaltered ideology, which simply couldn't accept any contact with institutions. The social centres split, between those who subscribed to the Milan Charter and those who didn't. The controversy was hard. They called us traitors and we called them pointless... maybe it's not completely decided, but now it's much softer. In those years we've shown that we didn't abandon the conflict, in fact the struggle has increased."

Another point of innovation and controversy was the relationship between the movement and the media. Hard lessons had already been learned about the way media attention can drag the focus of a movement away from its chosen terrain. When the Red Brigades emerged in the 1970s many activists thought it tiny and irrelevant compared to the size and vitality of the Movement

> **"We have to fight hard (and Genoa was a dramatic example) but we can't easily be pointed out as isolated thugs... They can talk about violence, radicalism, whatever, but they have to admit we represent a part of this society"**

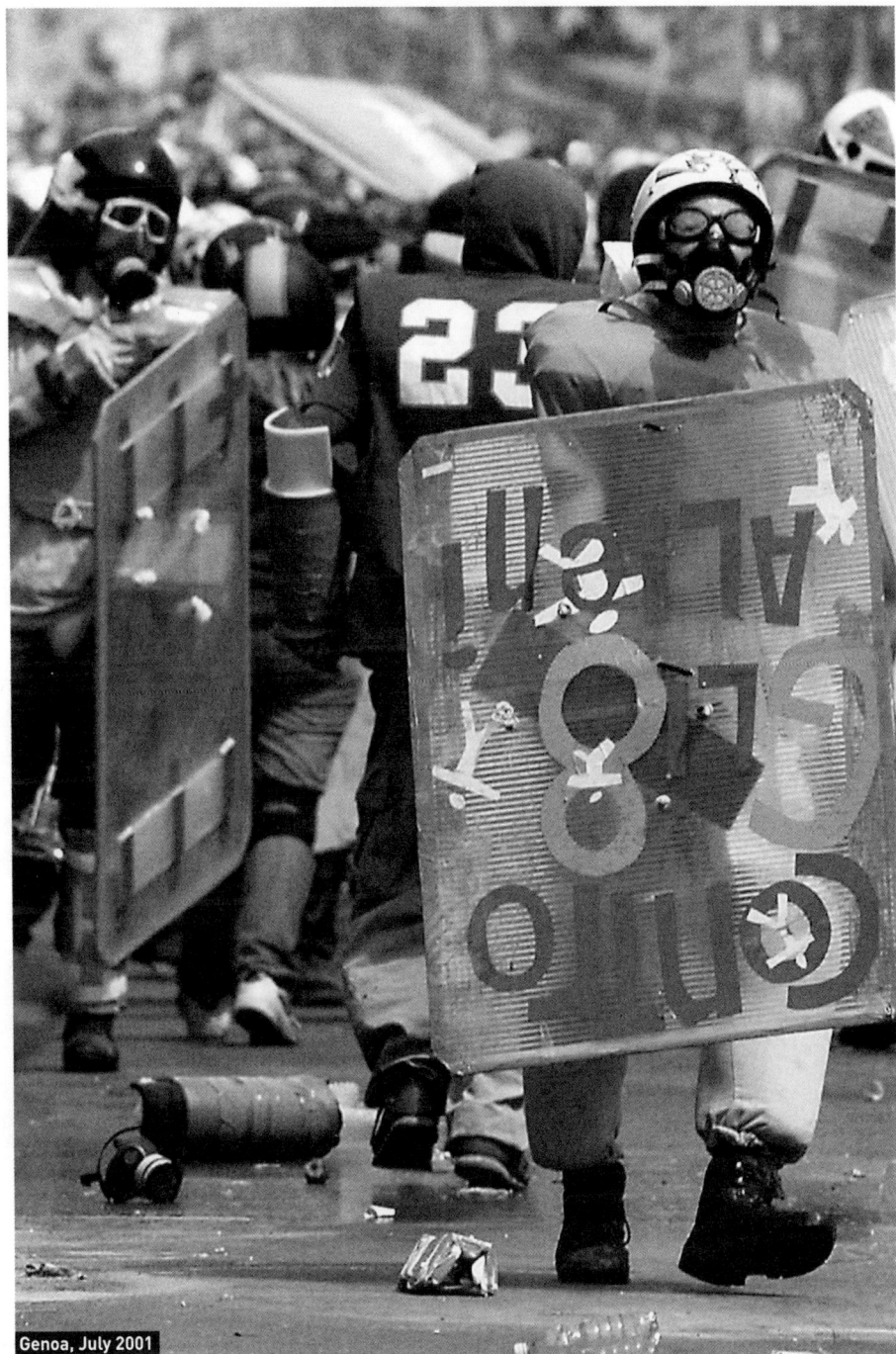

Genoa, July 2001

of 77. But terrorism acted like a media black hole, sucking in attention and setting the terms on which politics were seen and conducted. The essential point was that we don't exist outside the media and we must be in charge of our relations with it.

Protected demos had shields and padding but no offensive weapons. Their tactics were transparent. The ridiculous foam padding meant that they could only push and use weight of numbers – this made it obvious that any violence must come from the police. In fact looking ridiculous, disrupting expectations and mixing up signals was a powerful tactic against the media. A popular Tute Bianche chant was 'Here we come, Bastards', here we come sung to the tune of 'Guantanamera' while advancing with open hands towards the lines of riot police. The unofficial Tute Bianche salute was waving a little finger at the police – a way of saying 'here it is, come and break it'.

Another tactic has been to manipulate the press. Luca Casarini, a Tute Bianche spokesperson, has said: "We have analysts working on communication methods, we know what to do to make

PORTO ALEGRE, FEB 2002

GENOA, JULY 2001

people talk about us. If a journalist from *Il Giornale* (right wing newspaper) calls me and asks me for a headline I tell him: 'In Genoa we'll declare war on the powerful of the world', and he makes a headline out of it. Or else we spread the rumour of the mouse-men that are now digging galleries through Genoa's underground, and they buy it."

This was a dangerous game to play. A declaration of war made before Genoa backfired when the G8 leaders decided to reciprocate.

Genoa and beyond

The fruits of this new thinking are there to see in the innovative and expanding protest movement in Italy. The first successful padded demonstration was the storming of the Aviano airforce base during the Kosova war; other successes have included the dismantling of an immigrant detention centre, a water-borne protest against anti-immigrant naval patrols, and accompanying the Zapatistas on their glorious meander to Mexico City. But it's in the international counter-globalisation movement that the Tute Bianche's politics have really made

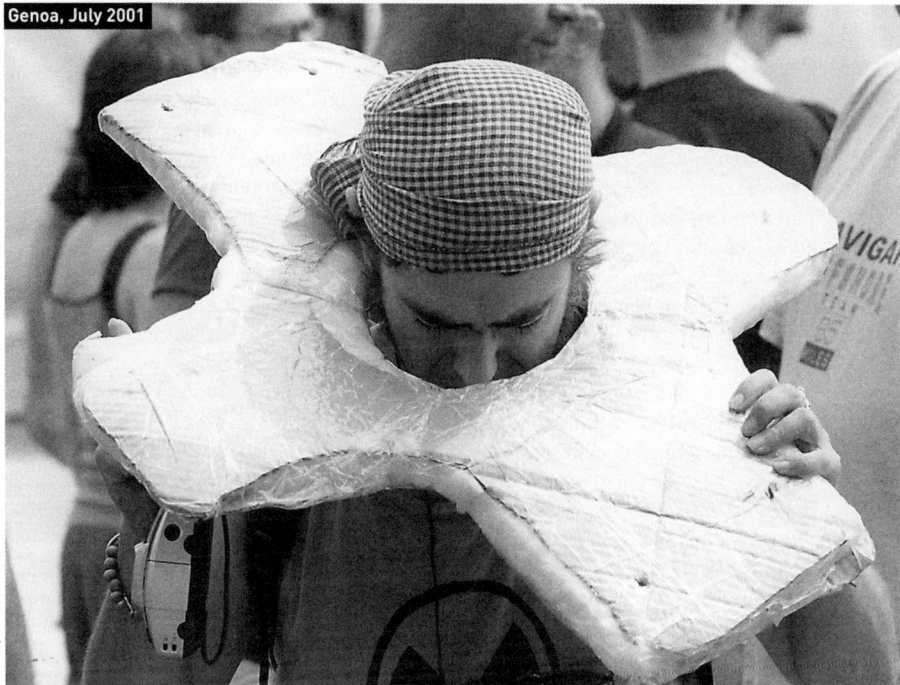

a mark. The sight of the mass ranks of Michelin men with shields and inflatables at the Prague anti-IMF demo brought the Tute Bianche to international attention. The anti-G8 protests on their home territory of Genoa were to be their biggest test. With 300,000 on the streets Berlusconi responded with escalating violence. Defensive shields were met with tear gas, indiscriminate beatings and armoured cars driven at speed into the crowds. Worst of all, Carlo Giuliani was shot dead and people were arrested and systematically tortured. It was time for a rethink.

"Padding and shields are not symbols but technical instruments to reduce pain. Sometimes it's better using them, sometimes not"

Before Genoa there had been a decision to take off the white overalls for fear they were becoming more of an identity than a tool: "The white overalls were a symbol," says Hobo. "It wasn't useful anymore. I think we have to never grow too attached to symbols, as they have their own cycle of life. Padding and shields are not symbols but technical instruments to reduce pain. Sometimes it's better using them, sometimes not. That's a technical choice."

The events in Genoa seemed to mark the end of a period of development. The Tute Bianche underwent a rethink and changed form. A new movement, the Disobedienti, was formed.

"This development is not just a rename, it's an expansion," explains Hobo. "Casting off the Tute Bianche also represented casting off a presumed role of leadership or avant-garde of a movement. The Disobedients are not only the social centres, they are a multitude composed of all who oppose neo-liberalism: many grassroots organisations, some catholics, sectors of parties... the whole range of people who were demonstrating in Genoa. It was time, especially at that moment, to give to this movement the strength to walk on its own legs. All together, all the different parts of mass movement. Thanks to this they couldn't pretend protest was confined only to those in the ghetto. All 'normal' people watching TV know the truth about the violence of the police."

A related but even more diffuse development has been the post-Genoa explosion of social forums across Italy. They are arenas where a wide range of civil society can meet and discuss.

"In each social forum there are social centres, grassroots associations, civic committees, student organisations, pacifist groups, Attac, Rifondazione Comunista (refounded communists), Verdi (greens party), Ya Basta, Cobas (radical trade union), sectors of CGIL (institutional trade union), Mani Tese (a catholic organisation), lila (aids activists), some gay associations, some independent media, etc. As for the general struggle, they brought the concept of generalised strike, meaning that the same rights should be extended to non-workers (students, unemployed, occasional workers, immigrants). There has been complete participation in the recent demos (including the general strike) in all the cities and in the social centres their presence has been very evident."

The problems being worked through are familiar to others in the counter-globalisation movement – experimenting with new forms of organisation that are relevant to the present. In Italy the buzz-word is the 'multitude', we'll let Hobo finish off:

"The 'multitude' concept came from a necessity to overcome the sectarianism of the former extra-parliament groups. The idea is to use networks just as capital does. The force of this movement is really in this networking method: a multitude, not a party. In time it has become a theory that led us to consider the force of difference. We think it's a winning notion, maybe the only way out." ✖

PRAGUE, SEPT 2000

HAU

Salzburg, June 2001

GOLCE & DABBANA

"They all must go!"

ARGENTINA ARDE AND ANDREW STERN

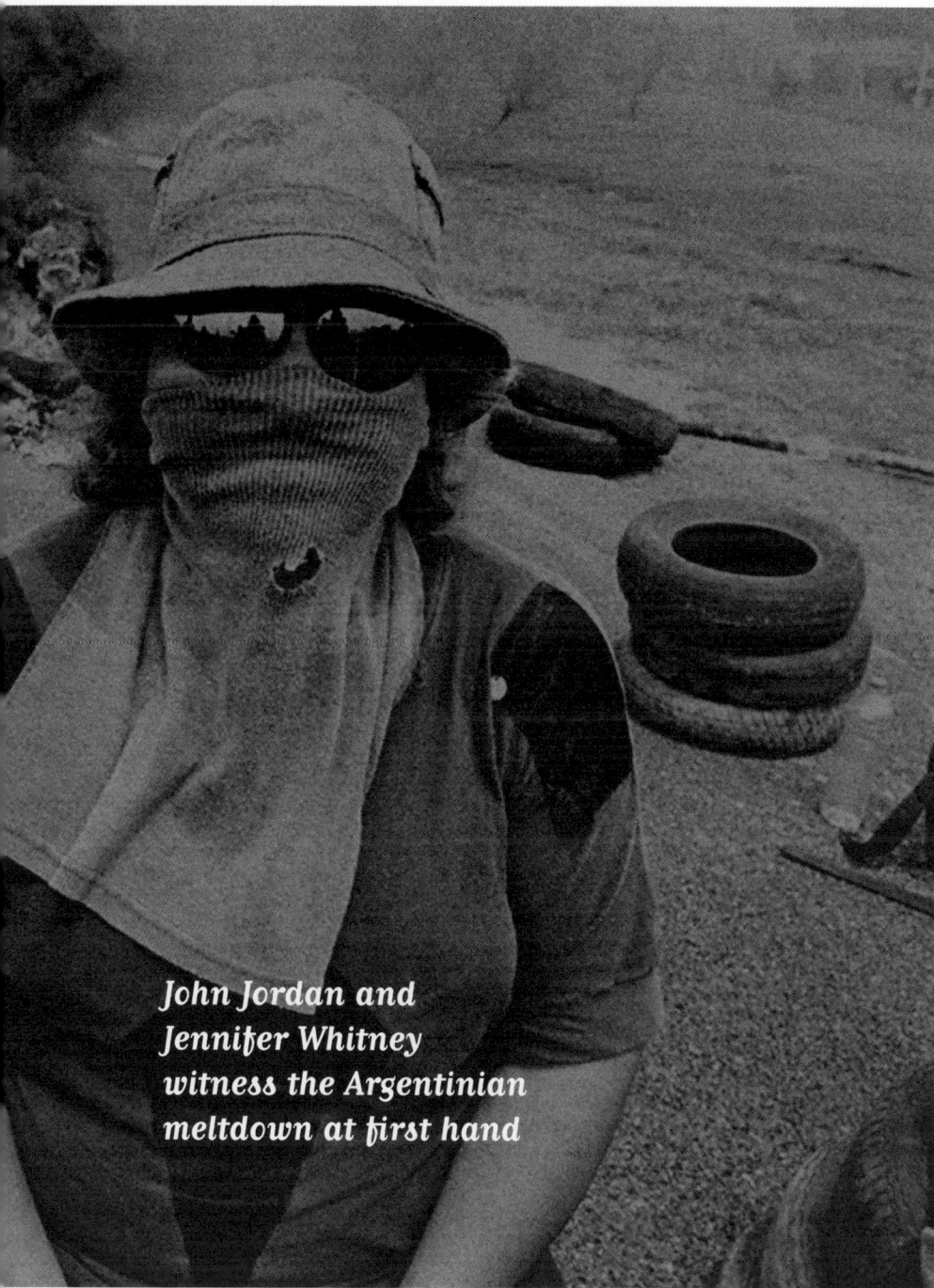

John Jordan and Jennifer Whitney witness the Argentinian meltdown at first hand

Routines and rebellions

15 February 2002 "Your tickets are invalid," says the heavily lipsticked agent at the Varig airlines check-in counter in southern Brazil. Her eyes flick to the next person in line. We protest vehemently, as we've had no problem using the tickets. She is not impressed, and calls for her manager, who explains to us that Varig no longer recognises the reciprocity of any tickets issued through Aerolineas Argentina. "They cannot be trusted now," she informs us gravely, showing us the memo announcing the new policy. "We no longer do business with them." This is our first experience of the rippling effects of the Argentinian financial crisis.

At the Aerolineas Argentina ticket counter, the agent is friendly, and seems a bit embarrassed. He books us tickets on the next flight to Buenos Aires. His demeanor suggests that of a man who does not know if he will have a job tomorrow. We board the plane, hoping that the massive layoffs and budget cuts have not reached air traffic control, aerospace engineering, safety inspection, and other related sectors. We arrive safely, get ourselves a cheap hotel, and bleary-eyed, head out for a coffee.

In the corner of the cafe a television with the volume down is tuned into the Cronica channel – a uniquely Argentinian phenomenon – non-stop live trashy 'news', seemingly unedited, with unbelievably bad and erratic camera work, and featuring the same lone reporter who seems to pop up all over town at random. Our introduction to Cronica is 'live and direct' scenes from the beach, complete with close-up shots of thongs which zoom out and reveal beach volleyball games and languid sunbathers. There's a massive social rebellion going on in this country, and the news is live and direct from the beach! After about 20 minutes of beach footage, it cuts to the news studio.

Two 'presenters' appear, in the form of shockingly pink-haired puppets! This is beyond ridiculous, here we are, desperate for news of the rebellion, and all we can get is puppet shows and thongs. After some 'live and direct' from the local football team's practice, we are finally rewarded with images of people banging pots and pans while invading the lobby of a bank. We quickly drink up our coffee, ask the waiter how to get to the financial district, jump on a bus, and arrive there in minutes.

Financial districts look much the same all over the world, whether in the City of London, New York, or Frankfurt, but here in Buenos Aires there is one major difference – huge corrugated sheets of steel cover many of the bank headquarters, especially the foreign ones, like Citibank, HSBC, and Lloyds. Gone are the grand entrance halls; the prestigious shiny surfaces of glass and marble are hidden behind blank facades of grey steel, and the only access is through tiny doors cut into the sheet metal, through which suited figures pass, heads bowed, entering these fortresses as if banking has become a secretive, clandestine activity.

The strong smell of wet paint hangs in the air, fresh graffiti covers the steel shuttering and walls, saying 'ladrones', or thieves. The action can't be far away. We split up and scout the area, listening for the clang of metal upon metal, the ineffable noise that has become the soundtrack to this rebellion, but hear nothing, find nothing. It seems that we are too late.

Economic freefall

We've arrived on a Friday. Every Friday night since mid-December last year, there has been a massive cacerolazo in Buenos Aires, when the people converge in the political centre of the city, the Plaza de Mayo, and create an enormous racket by banging on cacerolas, or saucepans. These huge cacerolazos developed spontaneously on the 19th of December 2001, the day when the uprising exploded, after smouldering in the provinces for several years, and now involving just about every sector of Argentinian society.

Argentina suffered two and a half decades of International Monetary Fund- (IMF) backed 'free-market reforms', which meant privatising everything: water, telephone systems, postal services, railways, electricity – you name it – even the zoo was privatised. When the Asian and Russian markets crashed in 1998, foreign investment dried up in the so-called 'emerging markets'. Argentina was hit badly, a major recession struck, and foreign lenders asked for their money back, on time.

According to the IMF, the only way the Argentinian government could repay the $132 billion debt, some of which dated from the military dictatorship, was by making more cuts in social spending, especially as many people, sick of political corruption, had stopped paying their taxes. Pensions, unemployment benefits, health care, and education all were cut drastically, and all state employees had their salaries slashed by 13%. It was the same old story repeated across the world – as countries are forced into deeper and deeper debt, the IMF strip-mines their economies for the benefit of foreign banks and bond traders.

In fact, it was the bond markets, unsatisfied with the pace of the austerity plans, who proved to be even harsher task-masters than the IMF. Unlike the IMF, they never bothered to send delegations to negotiate, they simply jacked up interest rates on debt issuances, in some instances from 9% to 14% in a fortnight. Now, after four years of recession, one out of every five Argentinians is unemployed, and some economists say this could soon double. Forty per cent of the population is now living below the poverty line, and another 2,000 people fall below it every day. Hospitals are running out of basic supplies like bandages and syringes, schools are shutting down because teachers aren't being paid, child mortality and hunger are on the rise, and this is all occurring in what once was one of the wealthiest countries in the world, for decades considered the great success story of neoliberal development in the 'developing' world, the star pupil of the 'Washington Consensus', and the main advocate for free trade in the region.

As the recession worsened, Argentinian stock plummeted, and the unpopular austerity measures became increasingly vicious. Protests spread further across the country. Things climaxed in December 2001 when, grasping for straws, the government decided to try a complicated re-negotiation of its debt repayments. Fearful that the entire economic house of cards was going to come tumbling down and that the currency would be devalued, thus wiping out their life savings, the middle classes panicked and withdrew about $135 billion from their bank accounts.

Fearing that a run on the banks would sink the economy, the detested finance minister, Domingo Cavallo, announced sweeping restrictions limiting the amount of money Argentinians could withdraw from their accounts. Known as the corralito, these measures included a monthly limit of $1,000 on cash withdrawals in addition to caps on off-shore transfers. With all the facets of the crisis interlocking, the economy was effectively paralysed. The IMF freaked out, due to the banking restrictions and the debt repayment plan, which would severely impact foreign banks, as they own 40% of Argentina's debt. They refused to lend any more money, and within weeks Argentina defaulted on its loans, the first time a country had done so in years. From this moment the economy was in free fall. On the 13th of December, a general strike called by major unions brought the country to a grinding halt for 24 hours. Six days later the popular rebellion exploded into the streets, where it remains today.

The tin pot insurrection

December the 19th was the turning point, the day when the Argentinian people said "Enough!" The stage was set the day before, when people began looting shops and supermarkets so they could feed their families. The president, Fernando De La Rua, panicked. Twelve years ago, major looting toppled the government, and now, within the Argentinian collective memory, looting is linked to the collapse of regimes. De La Rua declared a state of emergency, suspending all constitutional rights, and banning meetings of more than three people. That was the last straw. Not only did it bring back traumatic memories of the seven year military dictatorship which killed over 30,000 people, but it also meant that the state was taking away the last shred of dignity from a hungry and desperate population – their freedom.

On the evening of December 19th, our friend Ezequiel was on the phone with his brother who lives on the other side of Buenos Aires. They were casually chatting, when his brother suddenly said, "Hang on, can you hear that noise?"

ARGENTINA ARDE AND ANDREW STERN

Ezequiel strained to hear a kind of clanging sound coming through the receiver. "Yes, I can hear something on your side of the city but nothing here." They continued talking, and then Ezequiel paused, and said, "Wait, now I can hear something in my neighbourhood, the same sound... " He ran to the window.

People were standing on their balconies banging saucepans, were coming out on to the sidewalks banging pots; like a virulent virus of hope, the cacerolazo, which began as a response to the state of emergency, had infected the entire city. Before the president's televised announcement of the state of emergency was over, people were in the streets disobeying it. Over a million people took part in Buenos Aires alone, banging their pots and pans and demanding an end to neoliberal policies and corrupt governments. That night the finance minister resigned, and over the next 24 hours of street protest, plainclothes policemen killed seven demonstrators in the city, while 15 more were killed in the provinces. The president resigned shortly thereafter, and was evacuated from the presidential palace by helicopter. Within a fortnight four more governments fell. Argentina was now set on a major high-speed collision course, with the needs and desires of its people on one side, and the demands of the IMF, the inept government, and global capitalism on the other.

Rivers of Sound

15 February 2002 Our friends tell us to meet them for tonight's cacerolazo in the cafe of the Popular University of the Mothers of Plaza de Mayo. The place is an enormous social centre, right opposite the national congress building, and is run by the well-known mothers of the disappeared, whose courageous actions brought to the attention of the world the mass disappearances during the military dictatorship between 1976 and 1983.

Surrounded by shelves crammed with books, journals, and newspapers documenting radical Latin American political struggles, we drink the quintessential Argentinian drink of health and friendship, yerba mate, an extraordinary herbal infusion that increases energy and mental alertness and is believed to contain all of the

---

SICNOTES

NO DANCE; NO REVO...

So famous is the quote (rendered in a variety of ways), "If I can't dance, I don't want to be in your revolution," that it is even emblazoned on a souvenir coffee cup peddled by the Berkeley, Calif.-based Emma Goldman Papers project, and attributed to the turn of the last century anarchist, feminist, and free love advocate.

There's a problem with it, though. Two radical archivists with whom I checked couldn't find an authenticating citation for the quote anywhere in Goldman's voluminous writings and speeches, making its origins slightly suspect. But of all the words on thousands of pages written by Goldman about liberation and freedom, why does this perhaps fanciful quote remain the most prominent from her long career of fighting for anarchy?

Could it be that there is a human socio-biology that pulls us to the rhythms of dance, which even for a moment negate the straitjacket of authoritarian society with its thousands of rules meant to keep people within the rigid demands of the political state and capitalism?

In a decades old essay, 'The Decline of the Choral Dance', Paul Halmos describes how pre-capitalist people danced together as a community at ceremonies marking life's significant events, and often just for its joy. Such dancing disappeared as social activity with the rise of capitalist society.

Halmos saw choral dancing as invoking a "rhythmic communal rapture," a state of being in which the body experiences a sense of freedom and solidarity even when perhaps the mind doesn't. This emotional ecstasy prefigures the desire for revolution, and hence, is feared by rulers everywhere.

So, let's dance!

Peter Werbe

ARGENTINA ARDE AND ANDREW STERN

vitamins necessary to sustain life. The warm drink is served in a gourd with a silver straw and is passed around and shared between friends. No political meeting in Argentina is complete without mate, and some of us wonder whether this seemingly innocuous green twiggy tea is the secret ingredient behind this country's inspirational rebellion.

Night falls, and before long we begin to hear the repetitive rhythm of pot-and-pan banging drift across the square. A small crowd of around fifty people has congregated in the street – they are young, old, rich, poor, smartly dressed, scruffy, but all are armed with spoons, forks, and a whole variety of metal objects to hit: cooking pots, lids, kettles, Coke cans, car parts, biscuit tins, iron bars, baking trays, car keys. The rhythm is high pitched and monotonous, and above it people sing catchy tunes instead of dull political chanting; often they include the key slogan of this movement – que se vayan todos, they all must go – meaning that the *entire* political class goes, every politician from every party, the supreme court, the IMF, the multinational corporations, the banks – everyone out so the people can decide the fate of this economically crippled country themselves.

Our friend Eva tells us that the movement has lost some of its momentum over the last few weeks. We admit to being surprised by how small this crowd is – having imagined the cacerolazos to be enormous. But as we're thinking this, we reach a crossroads. To our right we see another crowd, perhaps twice as big as ours, coming towards us, waving and cheering. We continue for a few more blocks, and on the next street corner another stream of people flows out from the underground station, singing and jumping up and down as it merges with our group, another junction and yet more people come towards us. We began as 50, grew to a hundred or more, then we were two hundred, then five, then a thousand, two thousand, perhaps more. Rivers of people pouring into each other, growing bigger and bigger, rising to a roaring, banging torrent as we near the final destination, the Plaza de Mayo, where the presidential palace, the Pink House, stands protected behind police lines and barricades.

The neighbourhoods rise

Every week people make this pilgrimage, from every corner of Buenos Aires, some of them coming as far as seven kilometres. They walk with their asembleas populares, the neighbourhood meetings which have spontaneously sprouted up over the last few months in over 200 different neighbourhoods in the city, and throughout the surrounding provinces. These assemblies are rapidly becoming autonomous centres of community participation. Most meet weekly (the more ambitious, twice a week!), and all meet outside – in squares, parks, and even on street corners.

Every Sunday there is an assembly of assemblies, an inter-neighbourhood plenary in a park, attended by over 4,000

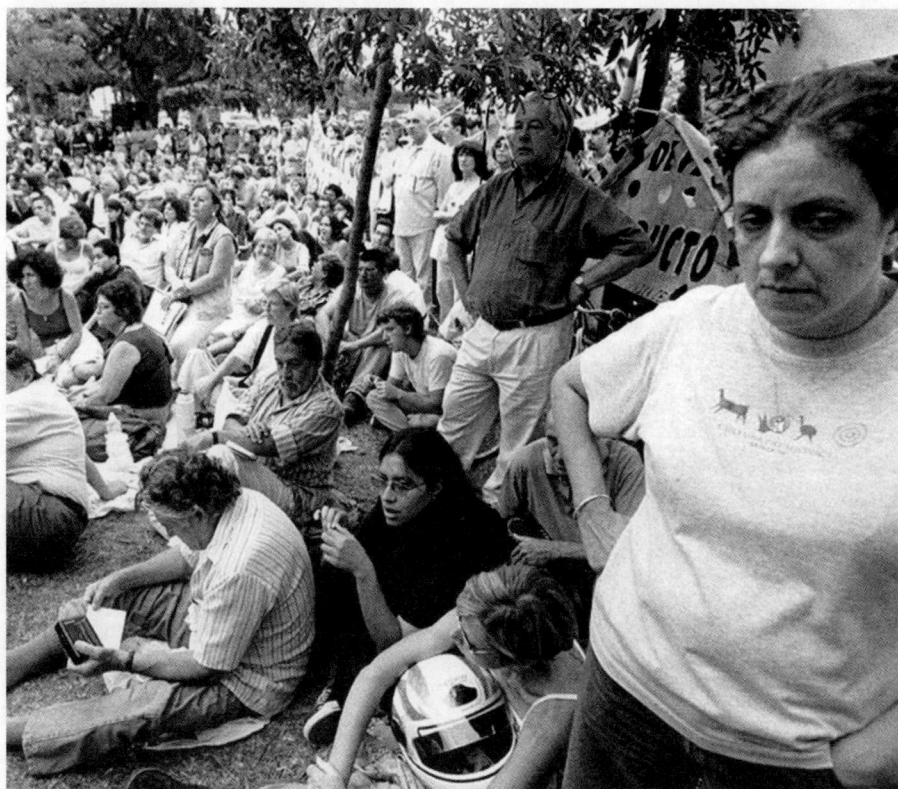

ARGENTINA ARDE AND ANDREW STERN

people and often running for more than four hours. Spokespeople from rich, poor, and middle class districts attend to report back on the work and proposals of their local assemblies, share ideas, and debate strategy for the following week's city-wide mobilisations.

The local assemblies are open to almost anyone, although one assembly has banned bankers and party activists, and others have banned the media. Some assemblies have as many as 200 people participating, others are much smaller. One of the assemblies we attended had about 40 people present, ranging from two mothers sitting on the sidewalk while breast feeding, to a lawyer in a suit, to a skinny hippy in batik flares, to an elderly taxi driver, to a dreadlocked bike messenger, to a nursing student. It was a whole slice of Argentinian society standing in a circle on a street corner under the orange glow of sodium lights, passing around a brand new megaphone and discussing how to take back control of their lives. Every now and then a car would pass by and beep its horn in support, and this was all happening between 8pm and midnight on a Wednesday evening!

It all seemed so normal, and yet was perhaps the most extraordinary radical political event I'd ever witnessed – ordinary people seriously discussing self-management, spontaneously understanding direct democracy and beginning to put it into practice in their own neighbourhoods. Multiply this by 200 in this city alone, and you have the makings of an irresistible popular rebellion, a grassroots uprising which is rejecting centralised political power. As Roli, an accountant from the Almagro assembly said: "People reject the political parties. To get out of this crisis requires real politics. These meetings of common people on the street are the fundamental form of doing politics."

Outside of the weekly meetings, the assemblies meet in smaller committees, each one dedicated to a different local issue or problem. Committees of health are common – with many local hospital budgets slashed, there is an urgent need to develop alternatives to the collapsing welfare system. Some are suggesting that people who own their own homes withhold their property tax, and instead give that money to the local hospitals. Many assemblies also have alternative media committees, as there is a widespread critique of the mainstream media's representation of the rebellion. It took a large cacerolazo outside their head offices to get them to cover the uprising more accurately. However, the spirit of distrust for any enormous corporate entity remains at large, and local assemblies are beginning to print their own news-sheets, broadcast updates on local radio stations, and put up websites.

In addition to the innumerable meetings and the weekly cacerolazo, the assemblies also organise local street parties and actions. In one neighbourhood, for example, the assembly organised pickets to prevent the authorities from closing down a baker who could not afford to pay his rent. For many of the assembly participants, this is the first time they have been involved in any form of grassroots mobilisation in their lives. By creating a space for people to listen to each other's problems and desires for change, the assemblies have enabled people to realise that their personal daily struggles are connected to other people's problems, and that all roads eventually lead to a similar source, whether it is the government, the banks, the IMF, or the entire economic system itself. An elderly shopkeeper, whose experience is representative of many participants, said, "Never in my whole life did I give a shit for anyone else in my neighbourhood. I was not interested in politics. But this time I realised that I have had enough and I needed to do something about it."

For radical change to occur, transformation has to take place in our minds as well as in social structures, and it is often on the tongue through the tool of language that one can trace some of the most radical shifts in consciousness. A beautiful illustration of this is that out of the experience of the assemblies, a new form of greeting has arisen. The traditional political leftist form of greeting in Latin American culture, compaero, or comrade, has been rejected in favor of a new form of address, vecino, or neighbour. It's a simple trick of the tongue, but one which signifies a major shift away from an authoritarian politics based on power and parties towards a participatory politics made up of people and places.

> **"Never in my whole life did I give a shit for anyone else in my neighbourhood. I was not interested in politics. But this time I realised that I have had enough and I needed to do something about it"**

Converging currents

15 February 2002 The raging torrent of sound finally arrives at the packed Plaza de Mayo. The mouth of each avenue feeding into the square is flooded with thousands of people cheering the arrival of each assembly. Banner after banner passes by, some roughly painted and others carefully lettered, but each bearing the neighbourhood's name and the time and place of the meeting. The repetitive metallic rhythm fills the night. Some people grow bored of hitting their pots and start to bang on lampposts or railings, others pound on the barricade which splits the square in half, behind which stand a symbolic row of riot policemen protecting the Pink House. Singing of the movement's anthem breaks out periodically, rising above the sound of the saucepans, voices crying, "They all must go, not a single one should remain, Duhalde must go back up his mother's cunt," sung with equal ebullience by elderly women, youthful punks, unemployed refinery workers, and middle class bankers.

Young kids are busy covering the walls with graffiti; hardly a surface of this city remains that does not carry some phrase or slogan of resistance. The outline of a coffin is drawn with the word 'politicians' inside; a ministry building proclaims 'My saucepan is not bullet proof'; the closed shutters of a shop declare 'Popular assemblies – go out into the streets and claim what is rightfully yours'. In the Plaza de Mayo, people are incredibly open, happy to talk with us, readily telling us stories, and repeatedly emphasising how important it is that we document their struggle and show it to the world.

The diversity of the crowd astonishes us – it seems that every walk of life is represented, and while we struggle to grasp the contradictions we perceive, we meet Pablo, a 30 year old employee of Bank Boston, who tells us, "By day I must work as a capitalist, but at night I'm a socialist. I've been a socialist for a long time, since my father was disappeared when I was six years old." His father was a university student of sociology, and was not particularly political, but was dumped in the Ro Plata all the same at age 22, leaving behind an 18 year old wife and his six year old son. It is this which is particularly poignant, the fact that every one of these people who is over thirty is living with some memory of the dictatorship, has lost some people from their immediate family (or at least knows someone who did) – they know how bad things can get, how disappearances serve to terrify a population in ways that we, with only prisons and courts as official deterrents, can't dream of.

This popular collective memory seems to permeate every aspect of this rebellion. Although the continuity of the lineage of resistance has been severely damaged, people seem deeply committed to doing the hard work of rebuilding a movement that was, until recently, in shambles, a movement that was long lulled to sleep by fearful memories not yet dulled by the passage of time, lulled to sleep by neoliberal promises and privatised dreams, convinced that without following the 'rules of the market', the country was sure to return to the dark days of dictatorship.

But not everyone is so sympathetic. "They had it coming," is a constant refrain from their Uruguayan neighbours, "They thought that they were European," and it's true that Buenos Aires feels much more like Paris than like Sao Paolo. However, the seemingly first-world status was propped up on credit and sustained by loans and a national refusal to recognise the symptoms of imminent collapse. Upon returning home, a Chicano activist tells us, "That's what's so important about the uprising. It's Latin Americanising Argentina. Argentina is remembering where it is on the map."

Time after time when we asked people in their neighbourhood meetings, or during cacerolazos, "Do you think that people here have participated in resistance movements in the past?" the answer was an emphatic no, often with the postscript that the near-complete loss of a generation through disappearance and exile meant that there were few people in the country with any prior experience of organising much of anything.

Extraordinary to imagine, and contrary to everything we thought we knew, to find that a people with so little foundation, so little affinity for each other, coming from such a place of apathy and individualism, followed by outrage and despair, could so rapidly and intuitively develop forms of organisation that are inherently disobedient, inherently directly democratic, and inherently utopian.

SICNOTES

When I was fifteen, I loved the diaries of Anaïs Nin. She was hopelessly glamorous. She lived in Paris... better (sounded more romantic), Neuilly... she was a writer, she had writer friends, she travelled by herself to exotic locations, she met on terms of perfect equality with men like Otto Rank, Rene Allendy, Henry Miller. Well... maybe not perfect equality. I was uneasily aware of a certain kittenish quality, a certain show-offy dependent little girl, in her work. In the interests of heroine worship, I ignored it.

I found out later that those diaries were a lie. Anaïs Nin was married through the entire time they take place, to a doctor, who apparently spoiled her rotten, and made possible her little glamorous starving artist pose. He took her to the exotic places. He paid for the typewriter she self-sacrificingly gave to Henry Miller, and probably replaced it immediately after. The whole thing, all the diaries, were one big pose. A little girl playing dress up.

I still remember how angry I felt when I found that out. And that anger was one of the most important moments of my growing up - not a bad inspiration at all.

Tod Davies

Although this scene in the Plaza de Mayo is repeated every Friday night, tonight's cacerolazo is special. For the first time, the piqueteros, or literally, picketers, will be joining the cacerolazo. The piqueteros are Argentina's militant movement of unemployed workers, who launched this social rebellion five years ago.

The power of the piqueteros

Born out of frustration with the corruption and constant political compromises of official unions and the failure of all political parties to represent them, the piqueteros (the term refers to their common tactic of road blockades) grew out of the excluded and impoverished communities in the provinces. They are predominantly unemployed workers who have been organising autonomously in their suburban barrios, the neighbourhood districts which are key to many Argentinians' sense of place and identity.

Demanding jobs, food, education, and health care, they began taking direct action in the mid-1990s, blocking highways across the country. The action of blocking the flow of commodities was seen as the key way to disrupt economic activity; as they were unemployed, the option to strike was no longer available to them, but by blocking roads they could still have an enormously disruptive effect on the economic system. One of them explained, "We see that the way capitalism operates is through the circulation of goods. Obstructing the highways is the way to hurt the capitalist the most. Therefore, we who have nothing – our way to make them pay the costs and show that we will not give up and die for their ambitions, is to create difficulties by obstructing the large routes of distribution."

"We block the streets. We make that part of the streets ours. We use wood, tires, and petrol to burn," adds Alejandro enthusiastically. He is a young piquetero who sports the red and black bandanna of the MTD (Unemployed Worker's Movement) around his neck and carries the three foot wooden club that has become one of the symbols of this movement. "We do it like this because it is the only way they acknowledge us. If we stood protesting on the sidewalk, they would trample all over us."

These tactics have proved extraordinarily successful. Whole families take part in the blockades, setting up collective kitchens and tents in the middle of the street. Many of the participants are young, and over 60% are women. Over the years this loosely federated autonomous movement has managed to secure thousands of temporary minimum wage jobs, food allowances, and other concessions from the state. The police are often unable to clear the pickets because of the popular support they receive. The highways often run beside shantytowns on the edges of the cities, and there is always a threat that any repression against the piqueteros would bring thousands of people streaming out of these areas on to the road in support, provoking much more serious confrontations.

In August 2001, a nation-wide mobilisation of piqueteros managed to shut down over 300 highways across the country. Over 100,000 unemployed workers participated and the economy was effectively paralysed. Thousands were arrested and five killed, but the movement continued building momentum and has broken new ground in its use of non-hierarchical grassroots forms of organising.

The spirit of autonomy and direct democracy that exists in the urban neighbourhood assemblies, was

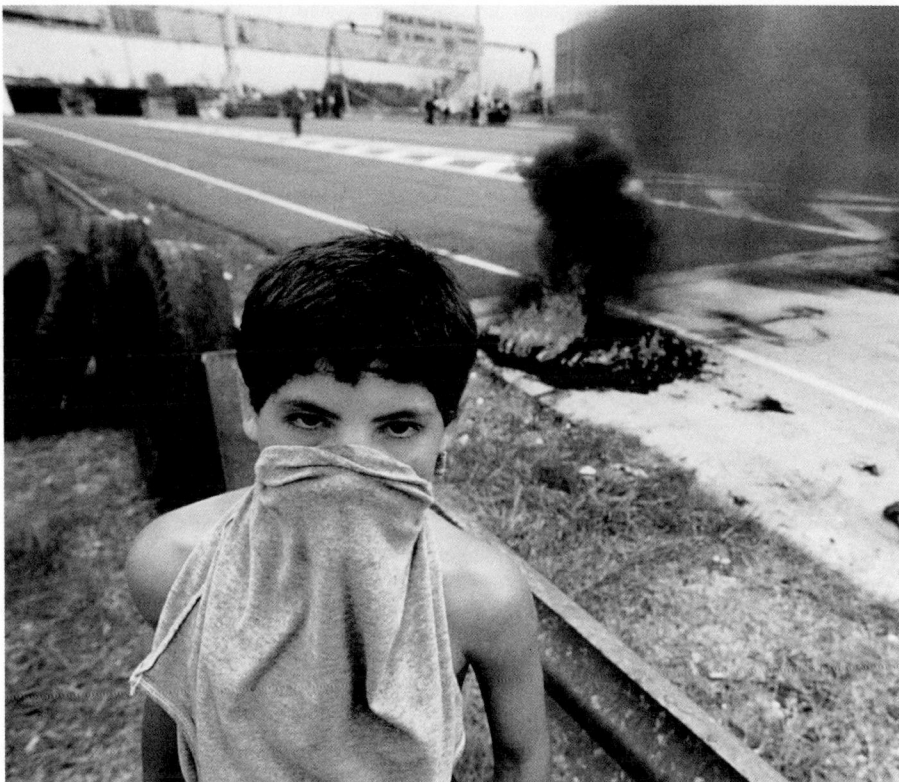

practised by the piqueteros years before, as they share a similar healthy distrust of all executive power. Each municipality has its own organisation centred around the neighbourhoods, and all decisions of policy and strategy are decided at piquetero assemblies. If the government decides to negotiate during an action, the piqueteros do not delegate leaders to go off and meet with government officials, but instead demand that the officials come to the blockades so the people can all discuss their demands, and collectively decide whether to accept or decline any forthcoming offers. Too often they have seen leaders and delegates contaminated, bought off, corrupted, or otherwise tainted by power, and they have decided that the way around this is

to develop radical horizontal structures.

The primary demands are usually the creation of some temporary state-funded jobs, and once these are secured, the piqueteros decide collectively who gets these jobs, based on need and time spent helping with blockades. If there are not enough to go around, they rotate the jobs and share the wages. Other demands normally follow: distribution of food parcels, liberation of some of the hundreds of jailed piqueteros, public investment in local infrastructure such as roads, health, education.

A friend shows us video footage of a passionate woman on last week's piquetero blockade of an oil refinery. She sits behind a barricade of burning tires, teeth missing beneath bright piercing eyes, and declares, "Yes this is dangerous, of course it is dangerous, but we need to fight, we cannot go home because no-one is going to bring anything to our doorstep... jobs, food for our children, the schools that are now disappearing, the hospitals... you see, if I get hurt now and I go to hospital, they don't even have the bandages to help me. So if we stop the struggle, all the things will disappear... we have to keep struggling."

In some parts of Argentina, the piqueteros have created quasi-liberated zones, where their ability to mobilise is far more influential than anything the local government is able to do. In General Mosconi, formerly a rich oil town in the far north, which now suffers with a more than 40% unemployment rate, the movement has taken things into its own hands and is running over 300 different projects, including bakeries, organic gardens, clinics, and water purification.

What is extraordinary is that these radical actions, practised by some of the most excluded and impoverished people in Argentina and using extremely militant tactics and imagery – burning barricades, blocked roads, masked-up demonstrators wielding clubs – have not alienated other sections of society. In fact, support comes from all across the movement. "When people get angry, they rule with blood, fire, and sweat," explains a young piquetero, wearing a 'Punk's Not Dead' t-shirt across his face as a mask. "We lost seven comrades in Plaza de Mayo. They had no political banner or ideology, they were only young Argentinians and wanted freedom. Then the government understood that people wanted to kick them out... Those that are up there in power are very worried that they can no longer order us around as before. Now people say 'enough'. We got together all social classes, from workers to unemployed, to say 'enough is enough', together with people that have $100,000 and that can't take it out of the bank, people that broke their backs working to save up, together with us that maybe don't even have any food to eat. We are all Argentinians, all under the same banner, and don't want this to happen again." A young piquetera named Rosa puts it more succinctly: "When women no longer have the resources to feed their children, the government is coming down, no matter what type of government it is."

> "When women no longer have the resources to feed their children, the government is coming down, no matter what type of government it is"

La lucha es una sola

15 February 2002 Tonight, we are privileged to watch the different currents of this struggle as they converge in the Plaza de Mayo. Suddenly there is a commotion in the corner of the square, which ripples through the crowd as all eyes turn to witness the arrival of the piqueteros, heroic, like a liberating army entering the city. Masked-up, tattooed, and fierce, each carries a stick of iron or of wood, which they hold together to form a cordon around themselves. They are greeted with an enormous cheer as they flow into the square with an energy and attitude which is forceful, raw, and urgent. Fireworks explode over the crowd as the Mothers of the Plaza de Mayo come forward to greet them, their small elderly faces framed in the white headscarf bearing the name of their disappeared children. Rising above the crowd are the royal blue and white flags of the Mothers on one side and the wooden clubs of the piqueteros on the other. Framed by their trademark symbols, they embrace, and the night resonates with the chant from the entire plaza, "Piquete y cacerolazo, la lucha es una sola," picket and cacerolazo, the struggle is the same.

What we are seeing tonight is an incredible coming together of differences, a convergence that crosses so many boundaries of class and culture. It seems that every social sector involved in this rebellion is beginning to work together, and support each other. Revolutionary epochs are always periods of convergence – they are moments when seemingly separate processes gather to form a socially explosive crisis. Argentina is explosive right now – anything could happen – it's an enormous social experiment that could well prove to be the first great popular rebellion against capitalism of the 21st century.

By four in the morning the square has emptied. The crowd has slowly melted away, returning to their neighbourhoods, and the city is silent again. Clusters of young people sit around on the grass talking, drinking, smoking – it could have been any Friday night out, in any city, but for the people painting the plaza with the names of those killed in December, or the small group huddled over a mobile silk-screen printing press, taking turns printing dozens of t-shirts with the simple slogan 'yo decido' – I decide.

Politics without parties

16 February 2002 We wake up the next morning to hear that the Pope has declared Argentina to be in a "pre-

anarchic" situation. He seems to be following in the footsteps of President Duhalde, who in the first week of February said, "Argentina is on the brink of anarchy." Weeks later, the finance minister chimes in, telling a meeting of international bankers, "Either we have continuity or anarchy." Funny how that word gets thrown around whenever power begins to feel threatened. It seems that they are using "anarchy" to conjure up the spectre of chaos, destruction, disobedience, nihilism, the collapse of law and order. It is doubtful they are using it to describe the authentic spirit of anarchism, which has spontaneously arisen on the street corners, and in the parks and squares of Argentina: the simple desire of people to live without rulers, remaining free to govern themselves.

What is so refreshing is that this spirit has developed so spontaneously, and that no-one, except a few tired old politicos (and the state of course), is using the word anarchism. This is perhaps surprising, given that Argentina had the world's largest anarchist movement at the dawn of the twentieth century. But no-one needs another 'ism' from the 19th century, another word which imprisons and fixes meaning, another word that seduces some people into the clarity and comfort of a sectarian box, and leads others in front of a firing squad or a show trial. Labels lead so easily to fundamentalism, brands inevitably breed intolerance, delineating doctrines, defining dogma, limiting the possibility of change.

From rebellion to reconstruction
There has been a clear pattern of rebellion against the IMF across the world over the last decades. From Indonesia to Nigeria, and Ecuador to Morocco, people have vented their

desperation and anger against austerity measures which have destroyed their livelihoods. Riots have erupted, sometimes the military is sent in, occasionally governments fall, but inevitably the IMF remains and austerity programs continue. Nothing changes, except for the growth of poverty and mistrust.

In the *Buenos Aires Herald*, we read a timely article about a new computer game called 'Playing Minister' in which you replace the Brazilian economic minister, and are charged with keeping the country on an even keel in the face of emerging market crises, domestic bank collapses and currency devaluation. The game, according to its creator, is designed to "test your skills at juggling interest rates, controlling inflation, balancing budgets and managing debts". Apparently managing the accompanying

health care crises and the food riots are not a part of the challenge when 'Playing Minister.'

During a recent interview, investigative journalist Greg Palast revealed how useful these riots are to the IMF. Palast relayed a conversation he had with Joseph Stiglitz, former chief economist of the World Bank: "'Everywhere we go, every country we end up meddling in, we destroy their economy and they end up in flames,' said Stiglitz. And he was saying that he questioned this and he got fired for it. But he was saying that they even kind of plan in the riots. They know that when they squeeze a country and destroy its economy, you are going to get riots in the streets. And they say, 'well that's the "IMF riot."' In other words, because you have riots, you lose. All the capital runs away from your country, and that gives the opportunity for the IMF to then add more conditions."

What the IMF doesn't expect and certainly doesn't want, is for people to take things into their own hands, for them to shift from resistance to reconstruction, from the desperation and rage of rioting to the joy of creating alternatives. As the economic crisis tears into the social fabric of Argentina, pushing more and more people to the edge, the tension between hope and despair becomes a conducive and creative space for change. Between laughter and tears exists the space of optimism, the space of radical social transformation.

For the workers of the Zann ceramics factory in Neuque, it is this spirit of optimism that has enabled them to occupy their factory, one of Latin America's largest ceramics producers, for the last six months, running it with astounding results. The company stopped production last year, claiming that it was no longer profitable and that they could no longer pay the workers' salaries. Rather than join the growing ranks of Argentina's unemployed, the workers decided to occupy the factory and keep the production lines running themselves.

"We showed that with two days' worth of production, we were able to pay the wages of all the workers for that month," explained Godoy, one of the 326 workers involved in the occupation, thus exposing the realities of where the company profits were really going. The workers market the tiles at 60% of the previous prices and have organised a network of young vendors who sell them in the city. Jos Romero, a maintenance worker at the factory, adds, "This fight has opened our eyes to a lot of things."

Like so many in this movement, they are critical of hierarchical forms of organisation. Godoy continues, "Now we have no full-time officials. The officials work eight hours like everyone else and we do our union activity after hours. The decisions are all made at general assemblies of workers, not behind closed doors." Photographs of the occupied factory show workers laughing and joking as they pull tiles out of the kilns. In Ursula Le Guin's extraordinary novel, *The Dispossessed*, which is perhaps the most tangible and touching description of an anti-authoritarian society in the English language, the word for work and play are the same. It seems the workers of Zann have begun to make this dream a reality.

Meanwhile, a mine in Ro Turbo has been occupied, as well as a textile factory in Buenos Aires, which recently opened its doors for an International Women's Day festival. These worker-run endeavours are setting examples for Argentinian factories everywhere, and perhaps setting precedents on ways of doing business in the 'new' Argentina. One manufacturer, who was on the verge of bankruptcy, called together his workers and told them that since he could no longer pay their salaries he would instead turn over blankets produced in the factory which the workers could either sell or take to the local barter markets, to exchange for other commodities. Perhaps he was worried by the example set at Zann, or perhaps he is beginning to recognise the futility of continuing business as usual in such unusual times.

Popular economics

16 February 2002 It is in the barter markets where another extraordinary example of necessity breeding ingenuity is enabling Argentinians to survive the crisis. We visit the Trueque La Estacin, or The Station Exchange, that takes place twice a week in a four storey community centre on the outskirts of the city, where we are shown around by Ana, a shy engineer wearing thick glasses. "The politicians have stolen everything from the people, they want to control everybody," she explains. "People come here because they don't want to be in the system."

The place is bustling; we can hardly move through the jovial throngs of people perusing the rows of tables offering goods and services. You can buy anything here, or rather, you can exchange anything here, from eggs to bumper stickers, miniskirts to spices, cucumbers to crocheted toilet roll holders, as long as you use the barter's own currency – small brightly coloured notes which look a bit like Monopoly money.

The system is simple: people take their products to the market and sell them for barter credit. The vendor is then able to use this to purchase products they need in return. If you have nothing to exchange and want to participate, you must buy credits from a bank with cash. But most people have something to trade, if they are imaginative enough, and though these people are deeply lacking in cash, they have a surplus of imagination.

Piles of bric-a-brac cover some tables, while others have neat and ordered displays. A young woman sits behind a pile of underwear reading Nietzsche while a mother carrying her child in a sling does a swift trade in home-baked pies. On one table Frederick Forsyth novels jostle for space with the Argentinian equivalent of *Hello* magazine and books about the Spanish Civil War. Huddled beside the stairs, an indigenous Bolivian family chat over wooden boxes of fresh vegetables. On the top floor a doctor in a pristine white coat offers to take our blood pressure, while a dentist demonstrates some procedure using a lurid pair of false teeth. People are having their haircut in one room while manicures and tarot readings are offered in another. There are classes in technical drawing as well as immigration advice. Occasionally the trueque radio station (which 'broadcasts' through a crackly PA system) announces new services being offered.

These barter clubs began in 1995, when the recession began to be felt. Since then they developed into a whole network and are now known as nodos, meaning nodes, or points of concentration. Currently there are several thousand nodos in existence throughout the country, with well over two million people taking part. For many of them it has become the only way of surviving the economic crisis.

SICNOTES

Being a young high school age sprout in the late 1960s, I had a headful of acid and lots of radical energy. But where I lived the game to play, in politics, was either the compromise solution of anti-war liberalism or a peculiar brand of really straight, anti-countercultural Trotskyism that happened to dominate the movement at the local university. So, on the one hand, I was dutifully studying Marx, Lenin, Fanon, and Mao. And on the other hand, I was tuning into Leary, Kesey, Huxley and Watts. But I was not seeing much connection between them.

Sure, I did read the underground press, so I was aware that a radical political counterculture existed. But nothing really brought it home for me until I read *Revolution for the Hell of It* by Abbie Hoffman. This wasn't so much a book as a psychic bomb, or maybe a laxative. It blasted the over-intellectualised shit away and energised me for the revolution.

Abbie's first book contained as much dadaist contradiction, poetry, and ruminations about the nature of consciousness as politics. With the possible exception of Hunter S. Thompson's *Fear and Loathing in Las Vegas*, it is still the most furious example of what spontaneous, unexpurgated writing can do. Read it if you can find it.

RU Sirius

As we leave the building we pass a stall-holder with whom we spoke during the afternoon, a strikingly tall, elegantly dressed woman in her mid-forties. She waves good-bye, her dark eyes filled with resigned sadness, in sharp contrast to the overall conviviality of the place, and her lips silently form the words, "We are hungry."

Beware the bourgeois block

18 February 2002 It's noon on a Monday, and we are on Florida Avenue, the main pedestrian shopping street of Buenos Aires, no different from London's Oxford Street, with its numerous McDonald's, Tower Records and Benettons. This busy street, normally full of bankers and business people making quick lunch-time purchases, runs along the edge of the financial district. But today something is not quite normal. The rustle of shopping bags is drowned out by a deafening racket.

A crowd of about 200 people are beating the steel sheet metal that protects the entrance of a bank. They bang with hammers, ladles, monkey wrenches, one woman even removes her shoe to use as a tool. The entire facade of the building shudders under the fury of the raining vibration of the blows. The force of some of the tools manages to punch gaping holes straight through the metal, agile gloved hands prise the sheets apart. Suddenly the armour falls away and the crowd cheers.

A handful of people split off and invade a bank lobby across the street. Within a fraction of a second all six ATM machines are systematically smashed, shattered glass flies, and a woman sprays the word 'chorros', or crooks, in huge letters on the marble wall. Nervous bank employees watch the scene from behind a glass door; an egg sails through the air and breaks against it. The bankers flinch, then turn away. The crowd repeats the accusatory chant, "Ladrones, ladrones," or thieves, and then join in a longer chant, while jumping ecstatically up and down, waving portfolios and briefcases around. The chant translates loosely as "Whoever is not jumping is a banker, whoever is not jumping is a thief... " When this dies down, everyone casually exits the lobby and moves on to the next bank, less than fifty yards up the street.

These kind of tactics have become archetypes of contemporary protest: the shattered glass, graffiti smeared across bank walls, the corporate symbols of capital destroyed. Images like these have been embedded in our imagination over the past few years, placed there by the mega-machine of mainstream media in its attempt to divide, discredit, and attack the growing anticapitalist movement, which is increasingly referred to as 'terrorist thugs', 'violent anarchists', and 'mindless mob'. From London to Genoa, via Seattle, Prague, and Quebec City, it has been the same story, the same images, the same rituals of symbolic destruction, played out over and over again; a high drama which effectively sells newspapers when splashed across the front page, and which serves to distract from the real issues at hand.

However, here in Buenos Aires, things are very, very, different. For one thing, it was impossible to tell the demonstrators from the passers-by. Men in suits and ties with briefcases in one hand and hammers in the other, women with gold bracelets, handbags, and high heels sharing cans of spray paint, anonymous suits on their lunch break joining the fracas and then melting back into the crowd. Walking through the pedestrian zone was astonishing – not only was it impossible to tell who was who, but also, businesses remained open, leaving their doors and windows open, fearless of looting or damage, as it was perfectly clear that the targets were the banks and nothing but the banks. Even McDonald's, usually having the honour of being the first to lose its windows, left their door open, solely guarded by the customary single private security guard.

Another major difference is that this is not the black bloc – in fact there are no hooded sweatshirts to be seen. No-one is masked, although one woman covers her face with a newspaper and large sunglasses, understandable if you've survived the disappearance of 30,000 of your fellow citizens. The spirit of

SICNOTES

WICKED: THE LIFE AND TIMES OF THE WICKED WITCH OF THE WEST
by Gregory McGuire
Ghalib says that since he was a wee tot, he's gravitated towards the wickedest ladies in fairytales – never for the distressed damsel, and not for more than a quick shag from the prince. It's a common phenomenon among queer boys, and *Wicked: The Life and Times of the Wicked Witch of the West* by Gregory McGuire answered our question of why.

Wicked is a re-telling of the Wizard of Oz, in which our heroine, the Wicked Witch of the West aka Elphaba, begins life as a sad green girl, hated by all. As the land of Oz becomes a fascist state run by a wizard/dictator, Elphaba becomes part of the anarchist underground, later re-emerging as an animal rights activist. In the process, we meet up with and take a new look at all the Oz characters... Glinda the Good, for example, is a snotty sorority girl who doesn't know how to reconcile her lash-fluttering, class-climbing aspirations with the fact that she has a heart, and a clue to boot.

As kids who have been branded as 'feminine' in an 'un-natural' despicable way, queer boys naturally align ourselves with the most despicable female character. There are thorns around the bubble of hetero bliss and 'normal' society, and they're rubbing up against us... We know the Witch is pissed, and we know why.

Wicked reminds us that history is in both the eye of the beholder and the hands of the oppressor, and that a much richer world exists beneath regular recorded history... it also reminds us how even the most 'progressive' among us can be thwarted when we cling to a narrow vision of what we want the world to look like.

Juha

'militant' (and often, macho) clandestinity is completely absent. It is broad daylight – while the bank is being trashed, shoppers are buying tennis shoes next door, and the handful of police, unable to do anything, stand idly, watching sheepishly. This is the most open, accountable, and disciplined property damage (one can hardly call it a riot when the police don't fight back) that we've ever witnessed. It's also probably the most surreal. If one must call these people a bloc – and why not, as they move and act as one – maybe 'bourgeois bloc' would suit them best.

The ahorristas, or savers, hold their demonstrations three times a week. On the day we followed them, 17 banks were 'visited'. Before meeting them, it was difficult to imagine women with shopping bags and high heels kicking at corporate windows, huge lipstick grins spreading as they watched the glass shatter into thousands of pieces. That day they also surrounded every armoured security van transporting cash from bank to bank that they came upon and covered each one in graffiti, while men in pin-striped suits proceeded to unscrew the wheel nuts and others pried open the hood, tearing out wires from the running engines. Soccer moms jumped up and down on top of the vans, smashing anything that could be broken, side mirrors, headlights, licence plates, windshield wipers and antennae. For three hours on a Monday afternoon, our understanding of the world was turned on its head, all our preconceptions and stereotypes melted away. "This could be my mom," we kept thinking.

The ahorristas are the upper to lower middle class who have had their life savings frozen by the government-imposed corralito. Dressed in shirts and ties, pumps and designer sunglasses, they just don't seem the sort who would be smashing up corporate property. They are architects, computer programmers, doctors, housewives, accountants, and even bank employees, one of whom, dressed in a business suit and holding a wrench and a metal bowl, explained, "It's not just the banks who are thieves, it's the government with the corporations. They confiscated the money we had in the bank. They stole it." She pauses, and then shakes her fist. "I am very angry!"

And yet the ahorristas are not simply the selfish petit bourgeoisie, worried only about their own money. Their struggle has broken out of the enclosure of self-interest, and has begun to encompass a critique of much of the social system. They have publicly allied themselves to the piqueteros and many take part in the assemblies. "A lot more than just the government must change here," says Carlos, a computer programmer, who has painted slogans all over his suit. His words echo those of the piquetero, Alejandro: "Us, the piqueteros, and all the people who are fighting, are struggling for social change. We do not believe in the capitalist neoliberal system anymore."

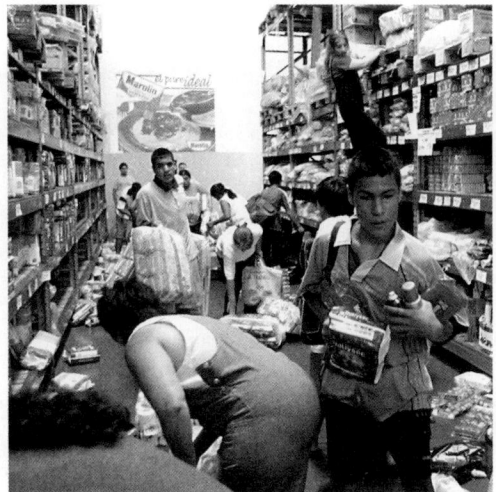

Predicting the unpredictable

"The repudiation of the politicians and the economic elites is complete," says Jos Luis Coraggio, the rector of a university in Buenos Aires who is active in the movement. "None of them who are recognised can walk the streets without being insulted or spat upon. It is impossible to predict what will happen. Next month, or next week, Duhalde could be deposed, we could be in a state of chaos, or we could be building a new country that breaks with neoliberal and capitalist orthodoxy."

Breaking with capitalist orthodoxy is what the IMF and the supporters of global capitalism most fear. Last year Fidel Castro caused a diplomatic storm when he accused Argentina of "licking the Yankee boot." Currently that boot is held over Argentina's face and will undoubtedly start kicking if the government does not find a way to please the demands of global capital, and get back to the business of licking again.

However, the government is between a rock and a hard place – even if it had an iota of legitimacy within Argentinian society, which it clearly doesn't, it could not possibly please both the hopes of the citizens and the demands of capital as enforced by the IMF. So what can it do?

Traditional remedies seem worthless, as the country's currency is steadily plummeting in value on the foreign exchange markets. People are queuing outside money changing shops for hours, desperate to change their pesos into dollars, before their cash becomes worthless. The government, in yet another desperate attempt to appear in control, put restrictions on the exchange rate, but this further infuriated the IMF because it is another artificial control of the markets. In response, Doug Smith, a Wall Street analyst, said, "The only thing that's going to stop this is for them to come up with some announcements that are credible and get the IMF behind them instead of trying to put Band-Aids on every situation." Yet there are no credible announcements to be made, and the wounds are too deep for Band-Aids.

A certain kind of language has become common currency recently. The head of the IMF, Horst Koehler, has declared that "... without pain, [Argentina] won't get out of this crisis." President Bush called on Argentina to make some "tough calls" before even thinking of the much-desired financial aid, and President Duhalde himself said that things are going to get a lot worse before they get better. Is this tough talk laying the groundwork for a military coup? After all, Argentina has had its fair share of these over the last century. But given the residual illegitimacy of the military, stemming from the decades of dictatorships, it seems that this option is unlikely, and besides, no-one wants to take power and inherit the current situation, not even the military. In fact, it seems that there may be dissent in their ranks – one officer told reporters, "Even if the situation turns to anarchy or civil war, if they ask me to intervene, my principal concern will be making sure my orders will be obeyed by my men."

More likely than another coup, or CIA-funded force invading to 'restore order' (common practice in Latin American history), another form of outside intervention will be attempted. "Somebody has to run the country with a tight grip," write two professors of economics in a *Financial Times* article brilliantly entitled, 'Argentina cannot be trusted'. The article goes on to suggest that Argentina "must surrender its sovereignty on all financial issues", it must accept "radical reform and foreign, hands-on control and supervision of fiscal spending, money printing, and tax administration," preferably from a "board of foreign central bankers," from "small disinterested countries." To phrase it another way, it would be like Belgian, Danish, and Swiss bankers coming in to run the British Central Bank and Inland Revenue Service.

Despite shocking poll results saying that 47% of the population agrees that large parts of Argentina's government should be entrusted to international experts, there is such distrust in banks that it seems unlikely that the arrival of more foreign bankers will calm people's nerves. As Enrique Garcia, president of the Andean Development Bank, said recently, "People in the streets feel that instead of being part of the solution, the banking sector is part of the problem."

The spirit on the streets and in the assemblies is that people can govern themselves. Another poll showed that one in three people had attended an assembly, and that 35% say the assemblies constitute "a new form of political organisation." The spirit of direct democracy and self-organisation has never felt as strong as it did as we watched the assemblies unfold in the long, warm Buenos Aires evenings. President Duhalde may say, "It is impossible to govern with assemblies," and believe that "the democratic way to organise and participate is through voting," but the people of Argentina have taught themselves through practice the real meaning of democracy, and the vacuous words of politicians now fall on deaf ears.

One evening, after attending his local assembly, a middle aged man who was active in the resistance against the military dictatorship, turned to us, and said in a soft, confident voice, "In the last month we have achieved more than we did in forty years. In four short weeks we have given ourselves enough hope to last us another forty years." So a choice does

exist, despite the government's blind adherence to the demands of the IMF. Argentina can choose between sovereignty and occupation, between the local desire of people and the global demands of capital, between democracy and empire, between life and money, between hope and despair.

Watch this space

15 February 2002 When we first landed in Buenos Aires, we were immediately searching for signs of the insurrection. Would this airport feel any different from any other? Would the streets be clogged with traffic, or with crowds? Was the garbage still being collected and the mail delivered? Never having been in a country in the midst of a mass social rebellion, we wondered what would appear different in everyday life. Riding into the city, we got our first clue. The barren stretches of highway that link cities with airports, so similar all over the world, are always flanked by rows of large billboards, advertising the staples of international business – Visa cards, mobile phones, hotels, airlines. This was true on this sterile strip of land, but something was different. Over half the billboards were completely bare, with huge white spaces where adverts would have been. There was something really beautiful about them, as they stood enormous in their emptiness, drained of the poisonous images of consumption, yet seductive in their nothingness, freed from commerce, and filled with possibility. They somehow stood for the space of change that this country is undergoing, they spoke of the pause, the blank sheet of paper waiting to be filled; they were the space from which a society could begin to imagine something different, the space from which people could begin to put dreams into action.

A postscript for the global anticapitalist movement

"Argentina's crisis is fast emerging as a sort of economic Rorschach test, used by economists and theoreticians of all ideological persuasions to prove their point," says the *Financial Times*. "Opponents of the 'Washington Consensus' say Argentina's experience

SICNOTES

GOD WAS A WOMAN
When was that dreaded day? Happy little baby trying to find his morning chores not even a year old. Briiiiinngg, briiiiinngg, briiiiinngg, 8am I'm in the kitchen by the phone, husband and baby a metre away. 'Yes doctor, no doctor we'll be there right away doctor.' ←head fuck→ A fretful walk across the park mummy, daddy, baby with new baby brother/sister on the way ←head fuck→

"Erm hum... I've never had to do this before, I'm so sorry ←head fuck→... erm hum, I don't know how to say this... the tests they – er we think it may be... more tests are needed – I'm sorry the cells... I'm sorry the cells... – carcinoma – I'm sorry the cells... ... CARCINOMA blah blah ←head fuck→ blah blah blah BlAh bLaH bLaH bLAh BlAh BlaH blah BlAh bLaH bLaH bLAh BlAh BlaH"←head fuck→...'CANCER'

"The sooner the better... we need you in straight away... are you 12 weeks? 14 weeks pregnant? We don't want it to go longer than 18 weeks"... "and what risk to the baby and what risk to me having more children..." "and what risk to the baby and what risk to me having more children..."

"what risk? ..." ←head fuck→...Will I stay alive for this little baby I hold in my arms now?

"Any advance on 18 weeks, we have19, yes,19 weeks from the surgeon in the corner 19

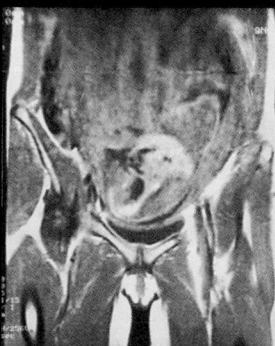

shows the perils of following the recipes of the IMF. Supporters of free markets say Argentina's experience shows the danger of not opening up [the economy] enough."

Argentina may well prove to be the crisis which irrevocably splits the ever-widening crack in the neoliberal armour, especially if things continue to unravel in other parts of Latin America. Recent events in Venezuela, and the possibility of left wing gains in this year's Brazilian presidential elections, point to a shift away from the 'Washington Consensus' across much of the region. The last decade has seen the increasing delegitimisation of the neoliberal model, as a movement of movements has sprung up on every continent, challenging the seemingly unstoppable expansion of capital. From Chiapas to Genoa, Seattle to Porto Alegre, Bangalore to Soweto, people have occupied the streets, taken direct action, practised models of self-organisation, and celebrated a radical spirit of autonomy, diversity, and interdependence. The movements seemed unstoppable, as mass mobilisations got bigger, more diverse populations converged, and the World Bank, WTO, IMF, and G8 were forced to meet on mountain tops, protected by repressive regimes, or behind fences defended by thousands of riot police. Seeing them on the defensive, having to justify their existence, gave the movements an extraordinary sense of hope.

By identifying the underlying global problem as capitalism, and by developing extraordinary international networks of inspiration in very short amounts of time, it felt almost as though history were speeding up, that perhaps we could succeed in the next phase, the process of imagining and constructing worlds which exist beyond greed and competition. Then, history did what it does best, surprising us all on September 11th when the twin towers were brought down, and it seemed for a while that everything had changed.

Suddenly hope was replaced by the politics of despair and fear. Demonstrations were called off, funding was pulled, and mass backpedalling and

any advance? Twenty weeks, yes 20 weeks from the professor stood at the front any advance on 20 weeks? Yes from you there sir: 21 weeks, final bit too, ah we have a rise from the surgeon to the right 22 weeks... "

"TWENTY EIGHT WEEKS the furthest we can possibly go 28 weeks... the baby will be fully formed lung capacity building AT LEAST a 50/50 chance of survival, YOU ARE a catholic."

"No, I am an ATHEIST and this is the worst day of my life, I just happen to believe all life is special all life deserves a shot I've HAD 27 years" ←head fuck→

A fretful walk across the park mummy, daddy, baby with new baby brother/sister on the way. It's 28 weeks. I'm deposited in a hospital bed father and baby leave, injections and advice ensue then intuition erupts and explodes through my heart head and mouth... I leave in my operating theatre gown and walk back through the same park. I want to stay pregnant forever my baby growing safely. It was a month before the arrival date, they HAVE to take the baby away from the incubated safety of my womb ←head fuck→

The scars appeared to heal as quickly as they grew, I'd wait on the end of a phone line simply waiting for God to tell me whether I was going to live or die, God was always a woman with a number of different dialects sat in a hospital office on the other end of my phone line. Had I not left in my operating theatre gown that day it emerged that they would have taken the baby away at 28 weeks. The direction of so many people's lives would have changed, some of whom were then in their own mother's wombs...

My little bundle of joy grew... and grew and continues to, grasping life with a sense of fairness and justice way beyond his years, inspiring all those close to him that surround him a decade later...

Although his older brother wouldn't always agree.

Tracey Sanderswood

distancing occurred within the movement itself. Commentators immediately declared anticapitalism dead. The editor of the *Guardian* wrote, "Since September 11th, there is no appetite for [antiglobalisation], no interest, and the issues that were all-consuming a few months ago seem irrelevant now." Others suggested that the movement was somehow linked to the terrorists. Clare Short, the UK development minister, stated that the movement's demands were very similar to those of Al-Qaida.

September the 11th forced a reappraisal among activists, particularly in the global North. It challenged us all to take a deep breath, put our rhetoric into practice, and think strategically, and fast. Then three months later, history seemed to resume its accelerated speed, when Argentina erupted, followed closely by the collapse of Enron. It seemed that despite the blindly nationalist, racist, and indefinite 'war on terror' to distract the world, neoliberalism was continuing to disintegrate. Perhaps the biggest challenge the global movements face now is to realise that the first round is over, and that the slogan first sprayed on a building in Seattle and last seen on a burning police van in Genoa, 'We Are Winning', may actually be true. The 'crisis of legitimacy' expands exponentially almost daily. Corporations and institutions such as the World Bank and the G8 are constantly trying to appease the growing global uprising, with empty promises of environmental sustainability and poverty reduction.

On May Day, 2002 a new book was launched by academics who lamented, "Today there is an anticapitalist orthodoxy that goes beyond a latent hostility to big business. It's a well-organised critique of capitalism." The book argues that we must "start standing up for capitalism" because it's "the best thing that ever happened to the world," and that "if we want to change the world then we should do it through business," and treat capitalism as a "hero, not a villain." Perhaps a few hours on the streets of Argentina, or a chat with former employees of Enron would show them the true villainy and absurdity of capitalism.

With mainstream commentators falling over themselves to declare that capitalism is good for us and will save the world, it seems clear that the first round of this movement has been a victory. There has been a "nearly complete collapse of the prevailing economic theory," according to economist James K. Galbraith. But the next round will be the hardest. It will involve applying our critiques and principles to our everyday lives; it will be a stage of working close to home. A stage where mass conflict on the streets is balanced (but not entirely replaced) with creating alternatives to capitalism in our neighbourhoods, our towns and cities, our bioregions. This is exactly where Argentina can show us an inspiring way to move forward.

The situation in Argentina contains many elements of the anticapitalist movements: the practice of direct action, self-management and direct democracy; the belief in the power of diversity, decentralisation, and solidarity; the convergence of radically different social sectors; the rejection of the state, multinational corporations, and financial institutions. Yet, what is most incredible is that the form of the uprising arose spontaneously: it was not imposed or suggested by activists, but rather, created by ordinary people from the ground up, resulting in a truly popular rebellion that is taking place every day, every week, and

including every sort of person imaginable.

Argentina has become a living laboratory of struggle, a place where the popular politics of the future are being invented. In the face of poverty and economic meltdown, people have found enough hope to continue resisting, and have mustered sufficient creativity to begin building alternatives to the despair of capitalism. The global movements can learn much in this laboratory. In many ways it is comparable with the social revolutions of Spain in 1936, of France in May 1968, and more recently, in southern Mexico, with the 1994 uprising of the Zapatista Army of National Liberation (EZLN) – all rebellions which inspired, then and now, millions around the world.

It was a spirit of innovative solidarity that sparked a transformation of the practice of politics, and led us into the first stage of this new evolution of people's movements. The Zapatistas sowed the seeds for creating 'rebellions which listen' to local needs and demands, and which are therefore particular to each place, and activists from around the world responded, not only through traditional forms of international solidarity as practised during the 1970–80s, particularly by Central American solidarity groups, but also through applying the spirit of Zapatismo by 'listening' at home. This network of listening that has occurred between many different cultures has been a cornerstone for the first round of this global movement, as it wove together its multiple differences, forming a powerful fabric of struggle.

Argentina has become a living laboratory of struggle, a place where the popular politics of the future are being invented

The second round needs to maintain these networks that nurture mutual inspiration flowing, because no revolution can succeed without hope. But the global anticapitalist movement also needs the reassurance of seeing its desires and aspirations being lived on a daily basis. The Zapatista autonomous municipalities in Chiapas are a kind of model, but are firmly rooted in indigenous culture, are small enclaves within a larger state, and are largely unexportable. Argentina, however, is an entire society undergoing transformation. It is a model that is much easier for the movements, especially those of the global North, to imagine occurring at home.

However, the movement in Argentina is in danger of isolation; without the security and the mutual inspiration of international solidarity, it will suffer greatly. The mainstream press has mostly ignored the situation since the December riots, and most people we met felt that the world was unaware of their plight. For once, no-one was chanting "The whole world is watching," because of course, it is in the interest of capitalism's defence team to ensure that we don't get to watch, don't get to see what's really going on. Although many anticapitalists worldwide have said "Thank God for Argentina," as we've had our hopes rekindled in the dark days post 9-11, most of the people on the streets of Argentina have no idea that they've provided such widespread optimism.

If Chiapas was the place from which the seeds of the first round of this movement blew, then Argentina could well be where those seeds land, begin to sprout, and put down roots. We need to find creative ways to support and learn from the rebellion there as we did with the Zapatistas. Some solidarity actions have been taken – the Argentinian embassy in London was occupied and an anarchist flag hung out front, cacerolazos have taken place from Seattle to Sao Paolo, Rome to Nairobi. A chant directed against the World Economic Forum when they met in New York, proclaimed, "They are Enron, we are Argentina!" But much more could be done, more stories could be exchanged, actions coordinated, and visits to the laboratory undertaken.

There is a joke currently circulating the Japanese banking community, that goes: "What's the difference between Japan and Argentina?" "About eighteen months." These bankers well know that the economic situation in Argentina will occur elsewhere, and that it is inevitable that the tug of war between people's desires for a better life and the demands of global capital will result in explosions across the planet. A recent report by the World Development Movement documents 77 separate incidents of civil unrest in 23 countries, all relating to IMF protests, and all occurring in the year 2001. From Angola to Nepal to Columbia to Turkey, the same cracks are appearing in the neoliberal 'logic', and people are resisting. A dozen countries are poised to be the 'next Argentina', and some of them may be a lot closer to home than we ever imagined.

We need to be prepared, not only to resist, but to find ways to rebuild our societies when the economic crisis hits. If the popular rebellion in Argentina succeeds, it could show the world that people are able to live through severe economic crisis and come out the other side, not merely having survived, but stronger, and happier for struggling for new ways of living.

As *Sic* goes to print, the economic crisis in Argentina continues to spiral out of control. Having succeeded in winning legal battles against the government (setting legal precedent that ricochets around the globe) and recovering their savings from banks, thousands of depositors are withdrawing their money from the banking system as fast as they can. More recently a judge has sent a police contingent and a locksmith to a branch of HSBC to recover a claimant's savings, while the vault of a branch of Banco Provincia was opened with the aid of a blowtorch. With the banking system about to go belly-up, the government decided to close all banks for an 'indefinite holiday'. When the IMF refused again to loan more money and the Argentinian congress threw out a bill that proposed converting the frozen bank savings into IOU government bonds, the new minister of economy resigned. In an emergency press conference, Duhalde declared, "Banks will have to open again and God knows what will happen then. Banks cannot be closed permanently. It would be absurd to think of a capitalist system without banks." It may be absurd to think of a capitalist system without banks, but it is equally absurd to believe in the continuation of the present global system. Perhaps the most realistic thing to imagine at the beginning of this already war-torn century, is a system free of capitalism, one without banks, without poverty, without despair, a system whose currency is creativity and hope, a system that rewards cooperation rather than competition, a system that values the will of the people over the rule of the market. One day we may look back at the absurdity of the present and remember how the people of Argentina inspired us to demand the impossible, and invited us to build new worlds which spread outwards from our own neighbourhoods. ✖

ARGENTINA ARDE AND ANDREW STERN

SIC PEOPLE

Argentina Arde and Andrew Stern
Argentina photography

Daisy Asquith
Film-maker
daisyasq@aol.com

Jake Black
Writer, journalist, poet and
member of Alabama 3

Johnny Brown
Writer and frontman with
The Band of Holy Joy

Colin Chalmers
Involved in *Schnews* and Simon
Jones Memorial Campaign
PO Box Brighton, 2600, BN2 2DX

Cynthia Connolly
Photographer, Discord
www.discord.com

Carolyn Coon
Artist, journalist and
founder of Release

Alex Cox
Film-maker
mail@alexcox.com
www.alexcox.com

Tod Davies
Script writer and film producer

Bill Drummond
Writer, half of KLF

El Vez
Performer, musician
http://members.aol.com/
elvezco

Mick Farren
Former member of the Deviants,
White Panthers and now a writer

Matt Fraser
Actor, performer, playwright

Matt Hannan
Member of 1 in 12 Collective
www.1in12.go-legend.net

Jeremy Hardy
Comedian, writer

John Jordan & Jennifer Whitney
artactivism@gn.apc.org
www.weareeverywhere.org

Juha
Queer Palestinian Hawaiian
hip-hop band
homoono@aol.com

Jon Langford
Member of the Mekons, artist

Rob Newman
Writer and comedian

Richard Niman
Artist

Danbert Nobacon
Member of the pop group
Chumbawamba
www.chumba.com

Norman
Activist, writer

Casey Orr
Photographer
www.caseyorr.com

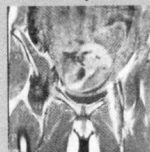

Tracey Sanderswood
Artist

Jon Savage
Writer

Warren Schnews
Schnews
"SchNEWS"
schnews@brighton.co.uk

R U Sirius
Mondo 2000, writer, social theorist
rusirius@well.com

Sivanandan
Novelist, essayist, activist
Institute of Race Relations

C J Stone
Writer

Swells
Journalist, writer, publisher

Mark Thomas
Comedian

Nick Toczek
Writer, performer and poet

Peter Werbe
Radio presenter, journalist,
member of *5th Estate* collective
www.peterwerbe.com

CONTACT
sic@chumba.demon.co.uk

Box TR666
Leeds
LS12 3XJ

SIC IS PRODUCED BY THESE SIC PEOPLE **KEIR MILBURN | BOFF WHALLEY | DUNSTAN BRUCE | ALICE NUTTER**